The Joy
of Music

LEONARD BERNSTEIN CONDUCTING

LEONARD BERNSTEIN

The Joy of Music

ANCHOR BOOKS

DOUBLEDAY

New York   London   Toronto   Sydney   Auckland

AN ANCHOR BOOK
PUBLISHED BY DOUBLEDAY
a division of Bantam Doubleday Dell Publishing Group, Inc.
1540 Broadway, New York, New York 10036

ANCHOR BOOKS, DOUBLEDAY, and the portrayal of an anchor
are trademarks of Doubleday, a division of Bantam Doubleday Dell
Publishing Group, Inc.

The Joy of Music was originally published in hardcover by Simon & Schuster in 1959. The Anchor Books edition is published by arrangement with the Estate of the Author.

Library of Congress Cataloging-in-Publication Data

Bernstein, Leonard, 1918–1990
The joy of music/Leonard Bernstein.
p.   cm.
    Originally published: New York: Simon and Schuster, 1959.
1. Music—History and criticism.   I. Title.
ML60.B47   1994
780—dc20   93-39504
CIP   MN

Grateful acknowledgment is made to Robert
Saudek and Mary Ahern for their invaluable
critical help in the construction of the *Omnibus* scripts, and to Henry Simon, the godfather
of this book, and Jack Gottlieb, my assistant,
for their excellent editorial assistance in preparing this book.

L. B.

CONTENTS

Introduction:

The Happy Medium

INTRODUCTION: THE HAPPY MEDIUM

EVER since I can remember I have talked about music, with friends, colleagues, teachers, students, and just plain, simple citizens. But in the last few years I have found myself talking about it publicly, thus joining the long line of well-meaning but generally doomed folk who have tried to explain the unique phenomenon of human reaction to organized sound. It is almost like trying to explain a freak of nature (whatever *that* may be). Ultimately one must simply accept the loving fact that people enjoy listening to organized sound (*certain* organized sounds, anyway); that this enjoyment can take the form of all kinds of responses from animal excitement to spiritual exaltation; and that people who can organize sounds so as to evoke the most exalted responses are commonly called geniuses. These axioms can neither be denied nor explained. But, in the great tradition of man burrowing through the darkness with his mind, hitting his head on cave walls, and sometimes perceiving a pinpoint of light, we can at least try to explain; in fact, there's no stopping us. *

There have been more words written about the *Eroica* symphony than there are notes in it; in fact, I should imagine that the proportion of words to notes, if anyone could get an accurate count, would be flabbergasting. And yet, has anyone ever successfully "explained" the *Eroica*? Can anyone explain in mere prose the wonder of one note following or coinciding with another so that we feel that it's exactly how those notes *had* to be? Of course not. No matter what rationalists we may profess to be, we are stopped cold at the border of this mystic area. It is not too much to say

* A shorter version of this Introduction appeared in the December 1957 issue of *The Atlantic Monthly*, under the title of *Speaking of Music*.

mystic or even *magic:* no art lover can be an agnostic when the chips are down. If you love music, you are a believer, however dialectically you try to wriggle out of it.

The most rational minds in history have always yielded to a slight mystic haze when the subject of music has been broached, recognizing the beautiful and utterly satisfying combination of mathematics and magic that music is. Plato and Socrates knew that the study of music is one of the finest disciplines for the adolescent mind, and insisted on it as a *sine qua non* of education: and just for those reasons of its combined scientific and "spiritual" qualities. Yet when Plato speaks of music— scientific as he is about almost everything else— he wanders into vague generalizations about harmony, love, rhythm, and those deities who could presumably carry a tune. But he knew that there was nothing like piped music to carry soldiers inspired into battle— and everyone else knows it too. And that certain Greek modes were better than others for love or war or wine festivals or crowning an athlete. Just as the Hindus, with their most mathematically complicated scales, rhythms and "ragas," knew that certain ones had to be for morning hours, or sunset, or Siva festivals, or marching, or windy days. And no amount of mathematics could or can explain that.

We are still, in our own day, faced with this magical block. We try to be scientific about it, in our bumbling way— to employ principles of physics, acoustics, mathematics, and formal logic. We employ philosophical devices like empiricism and teleological method. But what does it accomplish for us? The "magic" questions are still unanswered. For example, we can try to explain the "shape" of a theme from a Beethoven quartet by saying that it follows the formal principle of synthesis: that there is a short statement (thesis), followed by a "questioning answer" (antithesis), followed by a development arising out of the conflict of the two (synthesis). The Germans call this form *"Stollen."* Others say "syllogistic." Words, words, words. Why is the theme beautiful? There's the rub. We can find a hundred themes shaped in this way, or based on variants of this principle; but only one or two will be *beautiful.*

When I was at Harvard, Professor Birkhoff had just published a system of aesthetic *measure*— actually trying to evolve a mathematical system whereby any object of art could be awarded a beauty-rating on a given continuum of aesthetic worth. It was a noble effort; but when all is said and done, it comes to a dead end. The five human senses are capable of measuring objects up to a certain point (the eye can decide that "X" is twice as long as "Y"; the ear can guess that one trombone is playing twice as loud as the other); but can the senses' own aesthetic responses be measured? How far is the smell of pork from the smell of beans? What beans? Cooked how? Raw? In what climate? If the *Eroica* earns a grade of 3.2, what mark do you give *Tristan*? Or a one-page Bach prelude?

We bumble. We imitate scientific method in our attempts to explain magic phenomena by fact, forces, mass, energy. But we simply can't explain human reaction to these phenomena. Science can "explain" thunderstorms, but can it "explain" the fear with which people react to them? And even if it can, in psychology's admittedly unsatisfactory terminology, how does science explain the sense of *glory* we feel in a thunderstorm, break down this sense of glory into its parts? Three parts electrical stimulation, one part aural excitement, one part visual excitement, four parts identification-feelings with the beyond, two parts adoration of almighty forces— an impossible cocktail.

But some people *have* "explained" the glory of a thunderstorm — now and then, with varying degrees of success— and such people are called poets. Only artists can explain magic; only art can substitute for nature. By the same token, only art can substitute for art. And so the only way one can really say anything about music is to write music.

Still we go on trying to shed some light on the mystery. There is a human urge to clarify, rationalize, justify, analyze, limit, describe. There is also a great urge to "sell" music, arising out of the transformation of music in the last 200 years into an industry. Suddenly there are mass markets, a tremendous recording industry, professional careerists, civic competitiveness, music chambers of commerce. And out of this has come something called "Music Appreciation"— once felicitously called by Virgil Thomson the "Music Appreciation Racket." It is, in the main, a racket, because it is in the main specious and commercial. It uses every device to sell music— cajoling, coyness, flattery, oversimplification, irrelevant entertainment, tall tales— all in order to keep the music business humming. And in so doing it has itself become a business. The next step is obviously a new parasitic development— music-appreciation appreciation.

The "racket" operates in two styles, depending on the audience involved; and one is duller than the other. Type A is the birds-bees-and-rivulets variety, which invokes anything at all under the sun as long as it is extra-musical. It turns every note or phrase or chord into a cloud or crag or Cossack. It tells homey tales about the great composers, either spurious or irrelevant. It abounds in anecdotes, quotes from famous performers, indulges itself in bad jokes and unutterable puns, teases the hearer, and tells us nothing about music. I have used such devices myself: everyone who speaks about music at all must do it sometime or other. But I hope that I have done it always and only when the anecdote, the analogy, or the figure of speech makes the music clearer, more simply accessible, and not just to entertain or— much worse— to take the listener's mind *off* the music, as the Racket does.

Type B is concerned with analysis— a laudably serious endeavor, but it is as dull as Type A is coy. It is the now-comes-the-theme-upside-down-in-the-second-oboe variety. A guaranteed soporific. What it does, ultimately, is to supply you with a road map of themes, a kind of Baedeker to the bare geography of a composition; but again it tells us nothing about music except those superficial geographical facts.

Luckily all talk about music is not restricted to the level of music appreciation. There are writers in the learned journals who make sense, but only to other musicians, or to the cultivated amateur. The musical layman is harder put to find intelligent talk about music. But every once in a while a non-musician has appeared who has been able to give the layman some insight into music, if only into a cadence, or a melodic contour, or a single harmonic progression. Such people are rare and invaluable. Plato had some moments, as did Shakespeare. Certain critics can be perceptive and at the same time intelligible to the layman—

men like Sullivan and Newman and Thomson. Certain novelists, like Mann and Huxley, have turned out memorable paragraphs, or even chapters, on musical matters. But most novelists, and writers in general, tend to put their feet in their mouths whenever they part lips to speak of music. And they do it often. For some reason literary minds seem magnetized by musical terminology— probably because they are awe-struck by the abstractness of it all. Nothing can be more different from the representational literary mind, with its literal conceptuality, than the non-objective musical mind, with its concentration on shapes, lines, and sonorous intensities. And this fascinates the writer— makes him even a little envious, I have found— so that he longs for some participation in that strange, foreign medium. As a result, when he reaches for the elusive *mot juste* he often winds up with *glissando* or *crescendo* to express (usually wrongly) what he means— precisely *because* the musical word seems so elusive. Besides, it's so *pretty!* What chic and grace those Italian words carry with them! *Scherzo. Vivace. Andantino. Crescendo.* We are constantly running across the word *crescendo* in literature, almost always used synonymously with *climax.* "The storm rose to a great crescendo." "As they kissed, their hearts reached a crescendo of pounding passion." Nonsense. Obviously *crescendo* can mean only "growing," "increasing"— specifically, getting louder. So a crescendo can mean growing to a climax of storm or passion or anything you wish; but it can't be what you grow *to.*

This digression is only by way of pointing up the rarity of intelligent musical talk, even among first-class writers. The Huxleys and the Manns of this world are few and far between. Huxley's description of part of Beethoven's Op. 132 in *Point Counterpoint* is unforgettable, as is his paragraph on a Mozart quintet in *Antic Hay.* Mann has some thrilling passages on music in *The Magic Mountain* and in *Dr. Faustus.* And because of people like these— who can sometimes evoke with words the quality of a piece of music, or some sense of its essential weight or thrust— because of them we musicians are encouraged to go on trying to elucidate, in the hope that, even if only here and there, we can shed a little light on that terrible bugaboo, musical meaning.

"Meaning" in music has preoccupied aestheticians, musicians, and philosophers for centuries. The treatises pile up, and usually succeed only in adding more words to an already obscure business. In all this mass of material we can discern four levels of meaning in music:

1) Narrative-literary meanings *(Till Eulenspiegel, The Sorcerer's Apprentice,* etc.).
2) Atmospheric-pictorial meanings *(La Mer, Pictures at an Exhibition,* etc.).
3) Affective-reactive meanings such as triumph, pain, wistfulness, regret, cheerfulness, melancholy, apprehension— most typical of nineteenth-century romanticism.
4) Purely musical meanings.

Of these, the last is the only one worthy of *musical* analysis. The first three may involve associations which are good to know (if the composer intended them); otherwise they are concerned only with arbitrary justification, or prettifying for the commercial reasons mentioned before. If we are to try to "explain" music, we must explain the *music,* not the whole array of appreciators' extra-musical notions which have grown like parasites around it.

Which makes musical analysis for the layman extremely difficult. Obviously we can't use musical terminology exclusively, or we will simply drive the victim away. We must have intermittent recourse to certain extra-musical ideas, like religion, or social factors, or historical forces, which may have influenced music. We don't ever want to talk down; but how *up* can we talk without losing contact? There is a happy medium somewhere between the music-appreciation racket and purely technical discussion; it is hard to find, but it can be found.

It is with this certainty that it can be found that I have made so bold as to discuss music on television, on records, and in public lectures. Whenever I feel that I have done it successfully, it is because I may have found that happy medium. And finding it is impossible without the conviction that the public is *not* a great beast, but an intelligent organism, more often than not longing for insight and knowledge. So that, wherever possible, I try to talk about music— the *notes* of music; and wherever extra-musical concepts are needed for referential or clarifying purposes, I try to choose concepts that are musically relevant, such as nationalistic tendencies, or spiritual development, which may even have been part of the composer's own thinking. For example, in explaining jazz, I have avoided the usual pseudo-historical discussions (up-the-river-from-New Orleans) and concentrated on those aspects of melody, harmony, rhythm, etc., which make jazz different from all other music. In talking of Bach I have had to make references to his religious and spiritual convictions, but always in terms of the notes he produced. In trying to convey the problem of selection that confronts every composer, I have had recourse to actual rejected sketches for the first movement of Beethoven's *Fifth*. In other words, music appreciation doesn't *have* to be a racket. The extra-musical kind of reference can be useful if it is put in the service of explaining the notes; and the road-map variety can also be serviceable if it functions along with some central idea that can engage the intelligence of the listener. Therein lies the happy medium, which I humbly hope to have achieved in the pages that follow.

I

Imaginary Conversations

BULL SESSION
IN THE ROCKIES

SCENE I. WHY BEETHOVEN?

(Somewhere in New Mexico. Three of us are motoring at ridiculous speed to a destination, as yet unknown, in the Mad Mountains, Picasso Pass, or what you will. YOUNGER BROTHER, *sixteen, a licensed pilot and the world's authority on nuclear physics, is at the wheel, intent on overtaking every car on the road.* LYRIC POET, *on my left, is taut with terror and, I feel, is praying continuously for an immediate arrival, anywhere. He must live at least long enough to finish his current volume.* L.P. *is a poet's poet from Britain and one of those incredible people who are constantly so involved in politics, love, music and working ideals that, despite their established success, they often find themselves embarrassed in the presence of a laundry bill. When* L.P. *speaks, he is oracular; when he is silent, he is even more so.)*

L.P.
(With a certain frozen evenness): My dear Y.B., I suspect you have forgotten the fact that our tyreburst yesterday was caused by just such driving as you are now guilty of.

Y.B.
Don't end your sentence with a preposition.
> *(But Y.B. is impressed enough to reduce speed considerably— though gradually enough to preclude the suspicion that he has yielded a point. Few can impress hardboiled Y.B.; but even he is not immune to the oracle.*

Some minutes pass in relieved silence; and, with the tension gone, L.P. may now revert to the basic matter of all trip-talk: the scenery.)

L.P.

These hills are pure Beethoven.

(There is an uneventful lapse of five minutes, during which L.P. meditates blissfully on his happy metaphor; Y.B. smarts under the speed restriction, and I brood on the literary mind which is habitually forced to attach music to hills, the sea, or will-o'-the-wisps.)

L.P.

Pure Beethoven.

L.B.

(Ceasing to brood): I had every intention of letting your remark pass for innocent, but since you insist on it, I have a barbed question to put. With so many thousands of hills in the world— at least a hundred per famous composer— why does every hill remind every writer of Ludwig van Beethoven?

L.P.

Fancy that— and I thought I was flattering you by making a musical metaphor. Besides, I happen to find it true. These mountains *have* a quality of majesty and craggy exaltation that suggest Beethoven to me.

L.B.

Which symphony?

L.P.

Very funny indeed. You mean to say that you see no relation between this landscape and Beethoven's music?

L.B.

Certainly— and Bach's, and Stravinsky's, and Sibelius', and Wagner's— and Raff's. So why Beethoven?

L.P.

As the caterpillar said to Alice, "Why not?"

L.B.

I'm being serious, L. P., and you're not. Ever since I can recall, the first association that springs to anyone's mind when serious music is mentioned is "Beethoven." When I must give a concert to open a season an all-Beethoven program is usually requested. When you walk into a concert hall bearing the names of the greats inscribed around it on a frieze, there he sits, front and center, the first, the largest, the most immediately visible, and usually gold-plated. When a festival of orchestral music is contemplated the bets are ten to one it will turn out to be a Beethoven festival. What is the latest chic among young neo-classic composers? Neo-Beethoven! What is the meat-and-potatoes of every piano recital? A Beethoven sonata. Or of every quartet program? Opus one hundred et cetera. What did we play in our symphony concerts when we wanted to honor the fallen in war? The *Eroica*. What did we play on V Day? The *Fifth*. What is every United Nations concert? The *Ninth*. What is every Ph. D. oral exam in music schools? Play all the themes you can from the nine symphonies of Beethoven! Beethoven! Ludwig v—

L.P.

What's the matter, don't you like him?

L.B.

Like him? I'm all for him! In fact, I'm rather a nut on the subject, which is probably why I caught up your remark so violently. I adore Beethoven. But I want to understand this unwritten proscription of everyone else from the top row. I'm not complaining. I'd just like to know why not Bach, Mozart, Mendelssohn, Schumann—

Y.B.

Anybody want a piece of gum?

L.P.

Well, I suppose it's because Beethoven— or rather there must be a certain tra— That is, if one thinks through the whole—

L.B.

That's just what I mean: there's no answer.

L.P.

Well, dammit, man, it's because he's the best, that's all! Let's just say it out, unashamed: Beethoven is the greatest composer who ever lived!

L.B.

(*Who agrees, but has a Talmudic background*): *Dünkt dir das?* May I challenge you to a blow-by-blow substantiation of this brave statement?

L.P.

With pleasure. How?

L.B.

Let's take the elements of music one by one— melody, harmony, rhythm, counterpoint, orchestration— and see how our friend measures up on each count. Do you think it an unfair method?

L.P.

Not at all. Let's see, melody . . . *Melody!* Lord, what melody! The slow movement of the *Seventh!* Singing its heart out—

L.B.

Its monotone heart, you mean. The main argument of this "tune," if you will recall, is glued helplessly to E-natural.

L.P.

Well, but that is intentional— meant to produce a certain static, somber, marchlike—

L.B.

Granted. Then it is not particularly distinguished for melody.

L.P.

I was fated to pick a poor example. How about the first movement?

L.B.

Just try whistling it.

L.P. makes a valiant attempt. Stops. Pause.

L.B.

(*Brightly*): Shall we move on to harmony?

L.P.

No, dammit, I'll see this through yet! The . . . the . . . I've got it! The slow movement of the A-minor quartet! The holiness of it, the thankfulness of the convalescent, the purity of incredibly sustained slow motion, the—

L.B.

The melody?

L.P.

Oh, the melody, the melody! What is melody, anyway? Does it have to be a beer-hall tune to deserve that name? Any succession of notes— Y.B., you're speeding again!— is a melody, isn't it?

L.B.

Technically, yes. But we are speaking of the relative merits of one melody versus another. And in the case of Beethoven—

L.P.

(*Somewhat desperately*): There's always that glorious tune in the finale of the *Ninth: Dee-da-da—*

L.B.

Now even you must admit that one is beer hall par excellence, don't you think?

L.P.

(*With a sigh*): *Cedunt Helvetii.* We move on to harmony. Of course you must understand that I'm not a musician, so don't pull out the technical stops on me.

L.B.

Not at all, Lyric One. I need only make reference to the three or four most common chords in Western music. I am sure you are familiar with them.

L.P.

You mean (*sings*)

> "Now the day is o-ver,
> Night is drawing nigh;
> Shadows of the eeee-v'ning— "

L.B.

Exactly. Now what can you find in Beethoven that is harmonically much more adventurous than what you have just sung?

L.P.

You're not serious, L.B. You couldn't mean that! Why, Beethoven the radical, the arch-revolutionary, Napoleon, all that—

L.B.

And yet the pages of the *Fifth Symphony* stream on with the old three chords chasing each other about until you wonder what more he can possibly wring from them. Tonic, dominant, tonic, subdominant, dominant—

L.P.

But what a punch they pack!

L.B.

That's another matter. We were speaking of harmonic interest, weren't we?

L.P.

I admit I wouldn't advance harmony as Beethoven's strong point. But we were coming to rhythm. Now there you certainly can't deny the vigor, the intensity, the pulsation, the drive—

L.B.

You back down too easily on his harmony. The man had a fascinating way with a chord, to say the least: the weird spacings, the violently sudden modulations, the unexpected turn of harmonic events, the unheard-of dissonances—

L.P.

Whose side are you on, anyway? I thought you had said the harmony was dull?

L.B.

Never dull— only limited, and therefore less interesting than harmony which followed his period. And as to rhythm— certainly he was a rhythmic composer; so is Stravinsky. So were Bizet and

Berlioz. I repeat— why Beethoven? Are his rhythms more intriguing than the others? Did he introduce any new ones? Doesn't he get stuck on a pattern for pages, like Schubert, hammering it into your insides? Again I ask, why does his name, lo, lead all the rest?

L.P.

I'm afraid you're begging the question. Nobody has proposed that Beethoven leads all the rest solely because of his rhythm, or his melody, or his harmony. It's the combination—

L.B.

The combination of undistinguished elements? That hardly adds up to the gold-plated bust we worship in the conservatory concert hall! And the counterpoint—

Y.B.

Gum, anyone?

L.B.

— is generally of the schoolboy variety. He spent his whole life trying to write a really good fugue. And the orchestration is at times downright bad, especially in the later period when he was deaf. Unimportant trumpet parts sticking out of the orchestra like sore thumbs, horns bumbling along on endlessly repeated notes, drowned-out woodwinds, murderously cruel writing for the human voice. And there you have it.

L.P.

(In despair): Y.B., I wish I didn't have to constantly keep reminding you about driving sanely!

Y.B.

You have just split an infinitive. *(But he slows down)*

L.P.

(Almost in a rage— a lyrical one, of course): Somehow or other I feel I ought to make a speech. My idol has been desecrated before my eyes. And by one whose tools are notes, while mine are words — words! There he lies, a bedraggled, deaf syphilitic; besmirched

by the vain tongue of pseudocriticism; no attention paid to his obvious genius, his miraculous outpourings, his pure revelation, his vision of glory, brotherhood, divinity! There he lies, a mediocre melodist, a homely harmonist, an iterant riveter of a rhythmist, an ordinary orchestrator, a commonplace contrapuntist! This from a musician, one who professes to lift back the hide from the anatomical secrets of these mighty works— one whose life is a devotion to the musical mystery! It is all impossible, utterly, utterly impossible!

(There is a pause, partly self-indulgent, partly a silence befitting the climax of a heart-given tribute.)

L.B.

You are right, L.P. It is truly impossible. But it is only through this kind of analysis that we can arrive at the truth. You see, I have agreed with you from the beginning, but I have been thinking aloud with you. I am no different from the others who worship that name, those sonatas and quartets, that gold bust. But I suddenly sensed the blindness of that worship when you brought it to bear on these hills. And in challenging you, I was challenging myself to produce Exhibit A— the evidence. And now, if you're recovered, I am sure you can name the musical element we have omitted in our blow-by-blow survey.

L.P.

(Sober now, but with a slight hangover): Melody, harm— of course. Form. How stupid of me to let you omit it from the list. Form— the very essence of Beethoven, the life of those magnificent opening allegros, those perfect scherzos, those cumulative—

L.B.

Careful. You're igniting again. No, that's not quite what I mean by form. Let me put it this way. Many, many composers have been able to write heavenly tunes and respectable fugues. Some composers can orchestrate the C-major scale so that it sounds like a masterpiece, or fool with notes so that a harmonic novelty is achieved. But this is all mere dust— nothing compared to the magic ingredient sought by them all: *the inexplicable ability to know what the next note has to be*. Beethoven had this gift in a degree that leaves them all panting in the rear guard. When he really *did* it— as in the Funeral March of the *Eroica*— he produced an entity that always seems to me to have been previously written in Heaven, and then merely dictated to him. Not that the dictation was easily achieved. We know with what agonies he paid for listening to the divine orders. But the reward is great. There is a special space carved out in the cosmos into which this movement just fits, predetermined and perfect.

L.P.

Now *you're* igniting.

L.B.

(Deaf to everything but his own voice): Form is only an empty word, a shell, without this gift of inevitability; a composer can write a string of perfectly molded sonata-allegro movements, with every rule obeyed, and still suffer from bad form. Beethoven broke all the rules, and turned out pieces of breath-taking rightness. Rightness— that's the word! When you get the feeling that whatever note succeeds the last is the only possible note that can rightly happen at that instant, in that context, then chances are you're listening to Beethoven. Melodies, fugues, rhythms— leave them to the Chaikovskys and Hindemiths and Ravels. Our boy has the real goods, the stuff from Heaven, the power to make you feel at the finish: *Something is right in the world. There is something that checks throughout, that follows its own law consistently: something we can trust, that will never let us down.*

L.P.

(Quietly): But that is almost a definition of God.

L.B.

I meant it to be.

✷   ✷   ✷   ✷

SCENE II. WHAT DO YOU MEAN, MEANING?

(Later that day. The evening has begun to take hold of the "Bee-thovenesque" hills, mollifying them, planing them down to something more Chopinesque. Dusky rose-violet numbs the senses: we begin to hear the call of the tourist cabin, over the hum of the motor, to respond to the lure of the motel mattress. One yawn begets another, and there is presently a three-part moaning.)

L.P.

(Singing through his yawns):

> "Now the day is over,
> Night is drawing nigh;
> Shadows of the eev-ning . . . "

Y.B.

(Wiping away a tear): Anybody want a piece of gum?

L.B.

You know, I think I will, thanks. I talked myself dry in our last conversation. Gum, L.P.?

L.P.

Thank you, no. I don't chew. Besides, I didn't get the opportunity to talk *myself* dry.

(The effect of this blow is mitigated by the appearance on the roadside of the sign: "Transients," standing gray and inhospitable in the twilight.)

L.P.

Dare we investigate this twinkling hostel? Surround the groaning mead board? Bask in the glow of a genial host?

L.B.

You *are* getting tired. Maybe we'd better. Y.B., the honor falls to you. Descend and see if it isn't too haunted.

Y.B.

(Bitterly): Glad you trust my judgment. *(Stops the car and goes)*

L.B.

(Stretching): I feel as if I'd really done a full day's work.

L.P.

You did labor valiantly. That was a nasty piece of dissembling. Mediocre melodist, indeed!

L.B.

I admit I'm not much on dialectics; but strong feelings have a way of forcing the mind into curious channels. As a matter of fact, I haven't quite finished with you yet. Your innocent remark was really a double-edged sword, you know.

L.P.

Good Lord, what was it I said, anyway?

L.B.

(Stretching it out cruelly): "These-hills-are-pure-Beethoven." Remember?

L.P.

All too well. But I had thought, nay hoped, that we had kicked that one around until lost. What juice do you find left in this deathless phrase?

L.B.

Only this. It always seems strange to a musician when the literary mind begins associating music with all kinds of extra-musical phenomena, like hills and sprites and silver turnips. Funny, I haven't worried about these things since schooldays, when we battled out the singleness of artistic media in the aesthetics classroom; but your words have revived some old ghosts.

L.P.

You mean the ghosts of representationalism, abstraction, and so on?

L.B.

The same. Back at Harvard I had a remarkable roommate named Eisner who was well on his way to becoming a super-Hemingway. He had an unusual love for music, promiscuous and passionate, and I had a similarly constituted love for words. This led to a constructive relationship, as you can imagine, which taught us both a lot of half-truths. He died of cancer, dammit, shortly after graduation.

L.P.

I'm awfully sorry, but what does all this have to do with hills?

L.B.

Patience. Eisner and I used to have bull sessions almost nightly— thundering arguments that raged till dawn and made me miss my counterpoint class. Like all bull sessions, these never ended in resolution; but your remark today made me realize how deeply I had absorbed—

Y.B.

(*Returning to car*): Wow!

L.P.

You mean . . .

Y.B.

Very haunted. (*He starts up the motor*) Are you two at it again? (*Lurch*) You know it's very hard to see the road at this time of day (*second gear*), *entre chien et loup*, as they say at my high school (*third*), and your chatter doesn't help my concentration at all. (*Roaring speed*)

(*There is a stricken silence, during which one can almost hear Y.B. repenting in his soul. The tension grows, and bursts*)

Y.B.

(*Scowling*): What were you talking about, anyway?

L.P.

Damned if I know. Your dear brother was approaching some monumental height, as yet unnamed. He was telling of having absorbed something or other—

L.B.

(*Diving in*): Bull sessions! Thanks for the cue to re-enter. Well, naturally Eisner and I talked mostly sex and literature. But we almost always arrived sooner or later at the altar of music, and I was fascinated by his approach to it. Being a musician, and never having thought of being anything else, I had my own relation to music— quite unconsciously an abstract one— and I was amazed to find that another kind of relation could exist.

Y.B.

Typical sophomore.

L.B.

Just wait until you're one. But it was through Eisner that I first realized how different and foreign a writer's approach to music can be. You see, it would never occur to me to think of hills and Beethoven in the same breath. Music, of all the arts, stands in a special region, unlit by any star but its own, and utterly without meaning.

Y.B.

Even I would challenge that sophomorism!

L.P.

Bravo, chauffeur! Of all the idiocies—

L.B.

— without any meaning, that is, except its own, a meaning in musical terms, not in terms of words, which inhabit an altogether different mental climate.

L.P.

Are we embarking on a study of the meaning of meaning?

Y.B.

I sure hope not.

L.P.

Maybe we are. Let's see: what does a group of *words* mean, after all? For example, "She tilted her head and offered him her lips in surrender . . ."

Y.B.

A noble phrase.

L.P.

A knockout. But what does it *mean?* It means an action, a real action. And it entails a *re*action, a very real one. Something in your actual physical being responds to these dozen delicious words. And something in your physical being responds to a musical phrase as well— let's say the welling-up phrases in the *Liebestod.* Now what responds to one is the same element that responds to the other, isn't it? Ergo, the *meanings*— of both— insofar as meaning is what you, the perceiver, *have* after you perceive— the meanings of both are identical! Q.E.D.

L.B.

Bravo, Bishop Berkeley! Just like old academic times. I feel almost young again. Only I must object to your collegiate sophistry. In the first place, your logic is askew; you are confusing meaning with physical reaction which produces a false syllogism.

L.P.

Oh, come off it.

L.B.

No, really, I mean it. If I react similarly to two different stimuli, then my two reactions are the same; but that doesn't mean that both stimuli possess the same meaning. If a person catches cold 1) from rainy weather and 2) from cats, those facts certainly don't establish any similarity of meaning between rain and cats, do they?

L.P.

No, if we can head off a joke from Y.B. about raining cats and dogs. But this isn't a question of logic at all. Emotions don't follow mathematical patterns.

L.B.

I'm sorry, but weren't you the first to cry Q.E.D.?

L.P.

Very well, forgive me. But let's talk more simply. You will admit that there is a definite relation between the meanings of a sunset and of a Chopin prelude, between the Mona Lisa and the Book of Ruth, between—

L.B.

Relation, yes, in a comprehensive critical sense. But that is not to say that they *mean* the same thing.

L.P.

Of course it is to say *just* that! Take the sunset and the prelude, for example. We can break their meanings down into certain abstract terms, like calm, spaciousness, *sostenuto*, gentle motion, color, imperceptible changes of color, and so on. All these terms apply to both, don't they?

L.B.

But the prelude doesn't *mean* calm, color and the rest. It suggests them, perhaps. What it means is purely musical.

L.P.

And what does *that* mean?

L.B.

If it could be told in words, then why would Chopin have found it necessary to tell it through notes in the first place? Of course, I could try to articulate the musical meaning of a prelude in words, but what a bore it would be! Let me show you, if you have the strength: a prolonged upbeat in the middle register (like the A-string of the cello), yearning upwards in an octave stretch, its meaning suddenly clarified by the entrance of the accompaniment which is a series of repeated insistent E-minor triads that pulse under the sustained chromatic longing of the melodic line (which vacillates tearfully between B and C), while a tenor voice in the accompaniment adds to the general sense of languishing dolor through suspension and *appogiatura*—

L.P.

"Thanks, they cry, 'tis thrilling!
Take, O take this shilling!
Let us have no more!"

L.B.

See? I told you it would be a bore. And that may give you perhaps a fraction of the meaning of some three bars. That, as I said, is just the point about music. It stands in a special lonely region, unlit—

Y.B.

Hey, look! *Kozy Kabins!*

*   *   *   *

(The scene changes to the stoop of Kozy Kabin No. 8. It has be- come surprisingly cool, and we are sitting with blankets around us, three phony Indians, having that interminable last cigarette. We are on our fourth, at least; and the discussion of the meaning of meaning is raging.)

L.P.

— or else why do so many composers give their pieces titles? If you are right, then it is impossible for a piece of music to have any significance of a non-musical kind. Well and good. But then we will have to cut out of the history of music Berlioz, Strauss, Schoenberg, Hindemith—

L.B.

Mahler, Copland, Monteverdi—

L.P.

(Triumphantly): And Bernstein!

L.B.

Ouch! Now just give me a minute to dig back into my semester of aesthetics.

L.P.

I am positively glowing. We are waiting patiently. Have a Chester- field.

L.B.

(Stalling for time): As I see it, you want to know how I can follow such an abstract line in my theoretical view of music, and yet write pieces with names and philosophical implications and the like. Is that it?

L.P.

Only fairly well put. It's not that you are so all-fired abstract— how you flatter yourself! It just seems suspicious that you insist on such a mental purity about music, but don't give a hoot for purity when you write it. Intellectual snobbery, I call it. Of the lowest kind.

Y.B.

Olé!

L.P.

And now I will give *you* a lecture about music. And maybe I can say what you may have wanted to say, but in intelligible prose, and without varsity veneer.

L.B.

Yes, sir.

L.P.

Well, then. I think you want to get across that notes are opaque, and words are transparent, isn't that it? In other words, that when you read a newspaper you are not aware of the actual words themselves as an artistic medium; that the headline "Maniac Slays Six Ewes" conveys a concept, but does not linger in the consciousness with any particular value, am I right?

L.B.

Yes, sir.

L.P.

But that when these same words are in the hands of an artist, a poet, they can acquire a value of their own, over and above the mental image they convey; that words like "star," "would" and "steadfast" in the hands of Keats become memorable for their own sake as well as for the sake of the idea they represent, and that in so becoming they become less transparent, more opaque, more like *notes*, which exist basically for their own sake and not for any representational idea behind them. Are you with me?

L.B.

Yes, sir.

L.P.

That carried to the extreme, words thus handled can become almost completely abstract, as in the hands of a Gertrude Stein. Whether this extreme has any literary value is beside the point; the relevant fact is that words have their original function in representation, and are transparent; and notes have their original function in abstraction, and are opaque. And that, further, just as words can move in from that original function toward a middle ground of quasi-abstraction, as in Joyce, so musical notes can move in from their native habitat to the middle ground of conceptual meaning, as in program music, musical drama, background music, and the like. Do you follow?

L.B.

Yes, sir, but—

L.P.

Let me finish at least this one sally. So there is, after all, a common meeting ground for the writer and the musician, and neither one has cause or the right to glue himself fanatically to a snobbish purity-notion. And if we add to all this the God-given human capacity for association, there is no reason to carp at the spectacle of a simple Lyric Poet indulging himself a little sentimentally in a metaphor of hills and Beethoven. I grant you that the peroration of Sibelius' *Fifth Symphony*, in the most scientific sense, is only a particular succession of chords, scored in a certain sonorous way, producing the effect of a— well, of a peroration. But I have every right in the world to see a magnificent sunrise as I listen to these trumpets lighting up the sky with their orange streams of sound, and so would you if you would relax for a minute and forget your bookish notions. Dixi.

L.B.

I humbly agree with everything you say, and would gladly call it a night, and a cold one at that, except that I would like to make one suggestion. Perhaps our differences arise from the fact that the musician hears so much more in the music that he finds it totally unnecessary to bring associations into the picture at all. You and I, in our artistic disguises, do, as you say, come from opposite sides of the tracks, and can approach each other, meeting, so to speak, at the tracks themselves. But we always carry with us the heavy atavism of our origins, so that there is always the track itself separating us. We can never think identically about either words or music. These things are so subtle anyway that they can probably be made infinitely clearer in one happy line of poetry or one incommunicable flash of insight than in hours of shivering in this desert air. But I am grateful for your lecture.

L.P.

My, you are a considerably chastened young man, and a long way from the heckler of two hours ago. I congratulate you.

L.B.

And I you. I can't find a single chink in your disquisition. Although something tells me that if it weren't so polite, and I weren't so cold—

Y.B.

(Grimly waking up): To bed, to bed; there's a knocking at my head.

L.P.

I'll stay out a while longer with these incredible stars. Look at them, look at them! Aren't they pure Buxtehude!

(SUMMER 1948)

WHATEVER HAPPENED
TO THAT GREAT
AMERICAN SYMPHONY?

(The following, not properly a conversation, is an exchange of documents between L.B. and Broadway Producer, henceforth known as B.P., a man who interests himself, curiously enough, in some facets of art generally unknown to his calling. A born gentleman of average producer height; chin framed by a luxurious Persian-lamb collar which adorns his fifty-per-cent-cashmere evening coat; a man with an emerald tie pin and a wise, sweaty look— a man, in short, who carries his five feet two with pride and power.)

I. VIA WESTERN UNION

B.P.
HOTEL GORBEDUC
NEW YORK
VERY SORRY CANNOT ACCEPT KIND OFFER SHOW BASED BURTON'S ANATOMY MELANCHOLY SPLENDID IDEA WISH YOU ALL LUCK WITH IT REGRET UNABLE BUT DEEPLY INVOLVED WRITING NEW SYMPHONY GREETINGS

L.B.

II. VIA POST

L.B.
Steinway Hall
New York City
DEAR L.B.:

My associates and I were very much disappointed to receive your refusal by wire yesterday of our offer to collaborate with us, and with many other artists of outstanding merit and importance, on our new project for this season. I have long felt (and now feel corroborated by my associates in that opinion) that Burton's *Anatomy of Melancholy* would one day serve as the basis of a great work in the musical theater. We think that you are just the man to write the music for it, thereby enriching our stage which this season cries for such a work. Instead you tell us that you are writing a new symphony, a commendable enough enterprise. But if you will allow me to take a few minutes of your time, I should like to point out a few facts which you may not have taken into account in making your decision.

I begin with a question: why? Why continue to write symphonies in America for a public which does not care one way or the other about them? Can you honestly name me two or three people in all America who actually *care* whether you or anybody else ever writes another symphony or not? Do not answer this too hastily, or too defensively. The more you consider the question, the clearer will come the answer: that nobody, with the possible exception of some other composers and some critics who live by denouncing or flattering new works, will be any the sorrier if you or any of your symphonic colleagues never writes a symphony again. There seems to me to be no historical necessity for symphonies in our time: perhaps our age does not express itself truly through the symphonic form; I really am not in a position to know. I am a simple man, and know mainly through intuition whatever it is I know. I think I have my fingers on the pulse of the people, and believe me, L.B., it is not a symphonic pulse that I feel.

So there you are, writing music for which there is no historical necessity, probably; for which there is no public demand, certainly; and from which, if you will pardon me, there is no economic gain. Perhaps now you can see more clearly why I asked: why? Now let me ask: why not? Why not give of your talents to that sector of musical art in America where there is hot, live, young blood— the theater? Here you will find the public waiting for you, and you will be complying with the demands of history. All art, in all times, I believe, has been created to meet a public or private demand, whether it be the art of building Gothic cathedrals, or of painting the portrait of a wealthy patron, or of writing a play for the Elizabethan public, or of composing a Mass. Or, if you will again pardon me, the art of writing a symphony. Hadyn and Mozart and Brahms surely didn't write their symphonies in a vacuum; their symphonies were expected of them. Nobody today really *expects* a symphony of anybody. Our American composers have an obligation to the theater, which is alive and which needs them. Won't you think seriously about it again?

Faithfully,

B.P.

P.S. How had you planned for this new symphony to feed, clothe and house your charming wife and baby (to whom warmest personal regards)?

III. VIA POST

B.P.

Hotel Gorbeduc

New York City

DEAR B.P.:

I have read and reread your most interesting letter of yesterday, and I am impressed. I say *impressed* rather than *convinced*, since I cannot honestly report a change of heart as a result. But I have rarely met a producer operating in the Broadway area who has given so much sincere and deeply felt thought to a situation which basically does not concern his immediate livelihood. I am further impressed with your legal style, which is persuasive to a point where, if I were not more closely acquainted than you with the facts of the case (which is only natural), I might yield to your arguments. But the facts stand, and I feel obliged to report them to you.

There has never in history, by statistical record, been so great an interest in the symphony and in the symphony orchestra as is at this moment manifested in the United States. There are orchestras everywhere, in every small city, in every university and high school, in even some of our most provincial areas. How can you speak of "no public demand" when the latest figures of the League of Symphony Orchestras shows xx orchestras of major proportions now operating in the United States, as against xx orchestras of similar size in 19xx? The League further reports xx orchestras of smaller proportions now professionally active. Everywhere there have arisen festivals to which the public flocks in unprecedented numbers— and they are festivals which emphasize contemporary music almost as much as the standard repertory. Summer concerts have became as great an attraction as canoeing once was; and the winter seasons of our major orchestras are enjoying a lively increase in both attendance and interest. Community concert services send out great numbers of artists to cities large and small from coast to coast, where they are heard by audiences that a decade ago would not have dreamed of attending a concert.

I am sorry to bore you with statistics this way, but these facts are a matter of record. And think of all the new works being commissioned by such agencies as the Louisville Orchestra. xx works this year alone! And then think of the prizes, fellowships, awards of various kinds, all of which encourage the writing of concert music. Think of the enormous increase in the sale of records: why, it amounts almost to a craze. No, you cannot say that the public is indifferent to concert music. As to your reference to historical necessity, I simply do not understand you. And when you speak of economic gain, you are right; but economic considerations cannot enter into this area. One is an artist by necessity, and there are other ways of making money.

As you know, I love to write for the theater: I have done it before, and hope to do it often again. But this is a moment when other things come first. Thank you again for having asked me and for having taken the trouble to write.

Sincerely,

L.B.

IV. VIA POST

L.B.
Yaddo*
Saratoga Springs, New York
DEAR L.B.:
Forgive me for breaking into your privacy again, but in the week that has elapsed since I received your letter I have given a

* An artist's retreat.

lot of thought to the subject we have been discussing, and have even done some reading to back me up. Besides, your letter was so incredibly solemn, and, were it not for its obvious sincerity, so *dull*, if you will pardon me, that I am intrigued. I cannot believe that a young fellow like you, grown up in America, with the sense of fun that you have exhibited in some of your works, can possibly be such a fuddy-duddy. This letter is written partly to find out, and partly to acquaint you with my more recent thoughts about the symphonic form. I have given up the idea of trying to persuade you to do our show with us, and we are now negotiating with another composer. But you have awakened in me, by your refusal and your reasons for refusing, a real interest in this whole subject. I now have what might almost be called a theory. I explained it yesterday to our mutual friend P., who was in town for a day, and he found it silly. But what can you expect of a poet? As you know, he is also up at Yaddo for a month, working on his new volume, *Greaves of Brass,* and that's how I knew where to write you. Please avoid discussing my theory with him when you see him; his sense of historical necessity is appalling, if I can judge by the two poems from *Greaves of Brass* that he showed me yesterday.

Well, then, the theory. All music must begin in the theater, historically speaking. Does that amaze you? Just think about it. The origins of music are mostly folklore, comprising songs and dances of prayer, of work, of celebration, of love. This means that music first arises attached to words and ideas. There is no folk music, to my knowledge, that is abstract. It is music for working to, or for dancing to, or for singing words to. It is always *about* something. Then, as it develops, music becomes more sophisticated, more complicated; but it is still attached to concepts, as it is in the theater. Where music really grew up was in the church, wasn't it? The greatest theater of them all! (If ever there was theater music in the truest and best sense it was simple plain-chant.) Now we find little operas beginning to emerge, in Italy and in Germany and in Austria. The little operas (or masques, or singspiels, or whatever they were) become bigger operas— and we have Mozart. While in the church, little motets have grown into large requiems and cantatas. Now is the moment when the big switch can happen, and not until this moment. Now musical idioms have become familiar; and the procedures of Western music are enough alike so that the music can be *separated* from the words or the ideas or the concepts— that is, from the theater— and can exist for the audience in its own right. Now that there is a Mozart opera, there can also be a Mozart symphony. (But never forget that the symphony, as my books tell me, came from the opera overture!) And now that there are Bach Passions, there can also be Bach preludes and fugues. (But remember that the preludes and fugues were first of all reverie-pieces used in the church service!) In short, the audience had grown up *with* the music in the theater, and had reached the point where they could relate to the music *without* the theater. Their ears were ready for abstract sound: F-sharps and E-flats had become in themselves interesting and moving, without benefit of words to tell why they ought to be. But it had taken the audience a long time to reach this point.

Does all this sound like nonsense to you? I hope not: I'm banking on that solemnity of yours. But now to the meat of the theory.

The point I want to make with all my might is that America right now seems to me to be, musically, just about where Germany was around the seventeenth century. Deep in the singspiel. (We mustn't talk about present-day church music: that must be traditional, and has all been inherited.) But our secular music is just about where German music was fifty years before Mozart. Only *our* singspiels are called *Oklahoma!* and *Can-Can*. This is a period we must pass through before we can arrive at a real American symphonic form, or a real American style of whatever kind of concert music. It may not be the symphony as we have known it: we may produce something very different. But the musical language it will speak must first be created in our theater; then one day it can be divorced from "meaning" and stand alone, abstract. Do you see what I mean? For all our technical mastery and sophistication we are not really ready yet to produce our own concert music. As a result, all the stuff that is being turned out by the mile every day for concert performance in American halls is really European, and *old* European at that, with perhaps some American spice added by way of cowboy tunes or blues harmonies or jazz rhythms. But the music remains essentially European, because the whole notion of the symphonic form is a German notion, and don't let anybody tell you anything else. All the Russian symphonies are really German ones with vodka substituted for beer; and Franck's is German with some cornets making the difference; and Liszt's are German with nothing making the difference, and so are Elgar's and Grieg's and Dvorák's. Whatever national touches have been added, it's all German deep down, because the line of the symphony is a straight one smack from Mozart to Mahler.

Now here we are, remember, a brand-new country, comparatively speaking, a baby only a hundred and seventy-five years old. Which is nothing at all when you think of the old empires that produced that straight line I just mentioned. And actually we have been writing music in this country for only fifty years, and half of that fifty years the music has been borrowed clean out of the pockets of Brahms and Company. Of course we have the disadvantage here of having been born already grown up, so we don't start with folk dances and prayers for rain. We started with the leavings of the European development, handed to us on an old cracked dish. But then, we have an advantage after all: we have jazz. Which is the beginning of some other straight line which will grow here as certainly as the symphonic line grew out of another folk-strain for about a hundred years in Germany. Whatever jazz is, it's our own folk music, naïve, sophisticated, and exciting. And out of it has been born something we call the musical comedy. Well, 175 years isn't very long for that to have happened (and it really took only the last fifty years) compared to the centuries it took for the singspiel to arrive. And here we are at the point of building that singspiel into real opera— or, in our terms, developing *Pal Joey* into whatever American music is going to become. We are all ready and waiting for the Mozart to come along and just simply do it. That's why I'm in the producing business: I want to be there when it happens, if I live that long. I'm taking bids on the new Mozart. Any comers?

Well, there you have it. Very rough, not really thought out, but as plain as day to me. What I would love to make plain as day to you is the difference that arises out of all this between Europe and

America as they relate to concert music. A new Brahms symphony to a Viennese of that period was of consuming interest to him: it caused endless speculation about what it would turn out to be, how it would differ from the last one, and all the rest, just as we speculate now about a forthcoming Rodgers–Hammerstein show. It made table-talk the next morning; it was everybody's concern; it was part of daily living, the air breathed, food taken. As a result, the Viennese or German of today has inherited some of that possessiveness about the Brahms music: it is almost as though he had written it himself. The same is true of the relation between Italians and Italian opera. But in America the listener cannot share these feelings, no matter how wildly he loves the music of Brahms or Verdi, and no matter how much talk he makes about music being a universal language. There will always be the element of the museum about this repertory for him— the revered classic, always slightly remote. It can never be his private property, so to speak. And since he doesn't give a damn about whether anyone is writing new symphonies or not, there is no real vitality for him in our concert life, except the vitality of a visit to the museum. Q.E.D.

This has been a really long one, and I hope you will forgive my going on and on. But I was excited about this when it occurred to me and I wanted you to hear it all right away, even if you are trying to write that long, useless piece up there in your retreat. My best to P., and whatever you do don't let him talk you into setting *Greaves of Brass* to music. You're being abstract now, remember: you're committed.

Faithfully,

B.P.

V. VIA AIR MAIL

B.P.
Hotel Gorbeduc
New York City
DEAR B.P.:

It is a month since I had your last long, astonishing letter, and I apologize for my lateness in answering; but I have been to Yaddo and back to New York and then here to Milan all rather quickly. I had to suspend work on my symphony temporarily to fill this engagement conducting at La Scala, and now that the rehearsals and first performance are over I finally have a chance to answer you.

I must admit that I see to some extent what you mean about the sense of possessiveness toward music. Here in Milan people are still spending their time and energy at parties and luncheons arguing loudly about which is the greater opera, *Rigoletto* or *Trovatore*. As though it had all been written yesterday, hot off the presses. These Italians (or at least these Milanese) really own that music; and as you say, they seem to think they have written it all themselves. And you are right when you say that the wildest music-lover in the States can never relate that closely and familiarly to the same music. I am reminded of people at similar parties and luncheons in New York who will talk for hours about the relative merits of two hit musical shows, and even get excited or angry or hurt as they attack or defend them. All that part of your letter is perfectly true.

But I must take issue with your historical survey. It all sounds so easy and slick as you put it; and I admire you enormously for going into books and digging out all those facts and making them into ideas. Perhaps your main idea has some validity, but there are remarkable holes in your reasoning. What of the Frescobaldi *ricercare*, and the whole seventeenth-century school of organ music? What of Froberger and Pachelbel, who preceded Bach? Oh, all right, I'm being solemn and dull again, and I won't go into a lot of boring musicology. But you don't say the most obvious fact: that even if America is now in a period analogous to the singspiel period in Germany, she is at the same time equipped with the foreknowledge of the next 250 years. What a difference that makes, after all! Don't you see that the great development of German music was dependent on its very naïveté in its early stages? American composers can never be that naïve now, writing as they are after the world has already known Mozart and Strauss and Debussy and Schönberg. Perhaps they are condemned after all to be epigonous, and to follow in the line handed them by an already overdeveloped Europe. It may not be so exciting to compose now as it must have been in 1850; perhaps this is all very sad, but perhaps it is true. And anyway, what would you have all these serious American composers do? Go *en masse* into the shoe business? They are writing out of some sort of inner necessity, so there must be a real validity to it, whether or not it is explainable by your new theory.

I have a matinee today and so I must leave this and run to the theater. How is your show coming? Have you found a composer yet? I wish you luck and hope that whoever finally writes it will turn out to be your Mozart, in spades.

Sincerely,

L.B.

VI. VIA TRANSATLANTIC CABLE

LB

SCALA

MILANO

SHOE BUSINESS GOOD IDEA LETTER FOLLOWS GREETINGS

BP

VII. VIA AIR MAIL

L.B.

Teatro alla Scala

Milano, Italy

DEAR L.B.:

Hooray! You are a dead duck! You have obviously been convinced of my theory, and that makes me very happy. Your letter clearly shows that you have no real, sensible rebuttal. Of course what I said was full of holes; what do you expect from a brand-new musicologist? What do I know about Pachelbel and Fresco-baldi and that other guy? But what I know I know on all twelves, and at this point I am more certain than ever that I am right. Why, I went to the Philharmonic concert the other night, just to see what is happening in your thrilling concert world. There were empty seats everywhere. People were sleeping on all sides, some noisily, and I do not exclude one or two critics. It was all as dull as it could be, and the applause was polite and seemed intended more as something to start people's circulation going again after their nap than approval of the music. Dull, dull, dull! After the concert the audience shuffled out in a stupor, not talking much about it or about anything; and I shuffled to Sardi's for a double stinger. It was like waking up. The theater, the theater, on all sides: people arguing, recalling scenes and jokes with gales of laughter, people singing snatches of tunes to each other to prove some point, everyone alive. Alive, I tell you!

Sure, there are some American composers who will have to go on writing their symphonies which may get heard twice with in-difference. They may even be geniuses. I wish them all the luck in the world, and I hope they make it. But I have a sneaky feeling that they will continue to do symphonies because they *can't* do music for the theater. Don't think it is so easy to be a theater com-poser! In some ways it's harder: there is a discipline of the stage. You're not your own boss; it is the whole work that counts. A com-poser of symphonies has all the notes in the rainbow before him: he can choose as he wishes; not the theater composer. He really has to *work!* A great theater composer is a rare thing: he must have the sense of timing of a Duse, a sense of when to go easy and when to lay it on, a preknowledge of what the audience will feel every second of the work. He must have lightness and weight, wit and sentiment, pathos and brilliance. He must know his craft and everyone else's as well. Don't disparage him. I listened to *Tosca* the other day, and what a wallop it gave me! That man knew theater. And that man does not exactly languish in dishonor.

I tell you again: what is alive and young and throbbing with historic current in America is musical theater. And I tell you another thing: you know it as well as I do! You know in your heart that the real pieces of importance and interest to America now are not X's Fourteenth Symphony and Y's Flute Soliloquy, but *Finian's Rainbow* and *Carousel* and maybe even *Wonderful Town*, though I doubt it, and *South Pacific*. And all your long lists of dead statistics and all your Pachelbels put together cannot make you feel otherwise.

I want to thank you for giving me the push to go out and investigate all this stuff. I have never been so glad or so proud to be a producer of musical theater on Broadway. We are going ahead with our show at full speed, as soon as we find the right composer, and I can't wait to begin. I want to be part of this big new line that is forming to the right in the musical history of America, and I want to watch it take its place in the musical history of the world.

Faithfully,

B.P.

VIII. VIA TRANSATLANTIC CABLE

B.P.

HOTEL GORBEDUC

NEW YORK

PLANS CHANGED HAVE DECIDED ACCEPT YOUR SHOW STILL DISAGREE HEARTILY YOUR THEORY HOME NEXT WEEK WARMEST REGARDS

LB

(NOVEMBER 1954)

WHY DON'T YOU
RUN UPSTAIRS
AND WRITE
A NICE GERSHWIN TUNE?

(Through the windows of the English Grill in Radio City we can see the ice skaters milling about on the rink, inexplicably avoiding collision with one another. One cannot look at them for more than a few seconds, so dazzling are they as they whirl and plummet in the white winter sunlight. The shirred eggs are gone from our plates, and the second cup of coffee offers the momentary escape from the necessity of conversation. My lunch date with P.M. is one of those acid-forming events born of the New York compulsion to have lunch with one's business associates, at all costs, "some time," as if the mere act of eating together for ninety minutes were guaranteed to cement any and all relations, however tenuous.

P.M. is what is known in the "trade" as a Professional Manager, that unlucky soul whose job it is to see that the music published by his firm actually gets played. This involves his knowing, more or less intimately, an army of musical performers and some composers. He must once have been a large man, I think— powerful and energetic. He must have had young ideas and ideals. He must have gloried in his close association with the giants of the golden age of popular song-writing. But the long years have wearied him, and have reduced his ideas to formulas, his ideals to memories, his persuasive powers to palliatives. Still, he knows and loves two generations' worth of American popular music, and this gives him his warmth, his zeal, his function in life. I like him.

But why has he asked me to lunch? We have ranged all the immediately available subjects, and I feel there must be some-

thing in particular he wants to bring up, and can't. Everyone in the Grill seems to be talking, earnestly or gaily; only we remain chained to an axis of interest terminating at one pole in the skating rink and at the other in a cup of coffee. Again the skaters: back to the coffee. Compulsively, I break the silence.)

L.B.
How's business?
(This is inane, but he looks up gratefully. It must have helped somehow.)

P.M.
Business? Well, you know. Sheet music doesn't sell the way it did in the old days. It's all records now. The publisher isn't so much a publisher any more. He's an agent. Printing is the least—

L.B.
(Climbing on with excessive eagerness): But that ought to make good business, oughtn't it? The main thing is owning the music, the rights—

P.M.
Sure, but owning the music doesn't guarantee that we sell it. Take the music from your new show, for instance.
(So this is why he's invited me to lunch. But pretend innocence.)

L.B.
What about the show?

P.M.
(Kindly): How's it going?

L.B.
(As though this were just another subject): Fine. I caught it two nights ago. Seemed as fresh as ever.

P.M.
(Carefully): Very, very strange about that show of yours. It's a big success, the public enjoys it, it's been running for five months, and there's not a hit in it. How do you explain it?
(The bomb has dropped. The pulse has quickened.)

L.B.

How do *I* explain it? Isn't that your job to know? You're the man who sells the songs to the public. A hit depends on a good selling job. Don't ask me. I'm just the poor old composer.

P.M.

Now don't get excited. If you had been in this business as long as I have, you'd know that there are two sides to everything. There's no point in laying the blame here or there. A hit is the result of a combination of things: a good song, a good singer to launch it, thorough exploitation, and lucky timing. We can't always have all of them together. Now in your case, we've made one of our biggest efforts. I can't remember when we've—

L.B.

All right, I get it. You just weren't handed good material. I don't need a map. I don't write commercial songs, that's all. Why don't you tear up my contract?

P.M.

Really, L.B., you are in a state of gloom today. I didn't ask you to lunch to upset you. We all want to do our best for that score; it's to our mutual advantage. I just thought we might talk a bit about it, quietly and constructively, and maybe come up with something that might—

L.B.

I'm sorry. I'm somewhat sensitive about it. It's just that it would be nice to hear someone accidentally whistle something of mine, somewhere, just once.

P.M.

It's understandable.

L.B.

And I thought there were at least three natural hits in the show. You never hear the songs on the radio or on TV. There are a few forgotten recordings; one is on Muzak, I believe. It's a little depressing, you must admit.

P.M.

Now come on. Think of all the composers who don't have hits, and don't have hit shows either. You're a lucky boy, you know, and you shouldn't complain. Not everyone can write "Booby Hatch" and sell a million records in a month. Why, I remember George always used to say—

L.B.

George who?

P.M.

Gershwin, of course. What other George is there?

L.B.

Ah, but now you're talking about a man who really had the magic touch. Gershwin made hits, I don't know how. Some people do it all the time, like breathing. I don't know.

P.M.

(Plunging in): Well, now that you mention it, it might not be a bad idea for you to give a little thought now and then to these things. Learn a little from George. Your songs are simply too arty, that's all. You try too hard to make them what you would call "interesting." That's not for the public, you know. A special little dissonant effect in the bass may make *you* happy, and maybe some of your highbrow friends, but it doesn't help to make a hit. You're too wrapped up in unusual chords and odd skips in the tune and screwy forms: that's all only an amusing game you play with yourself. George didn't worry about all that. He wrote tunes, dozens of them, simple tunes that the world could sing and re-member and want to sing again. He wrote for people, not for critics. You just have to learn how to be simple, my boy.

L.B.

You think it's so simple to be simple? Not at all. I've tried hard for years. After all this isn't the first time I'm hearing this lecture. A few weeks ago a serious composer-friend and I were talking about all this, and we got boiling mad about it. Why shouldn't we be able to come up with a hit, we said, if the standard is as low as it seems to be? We decided that all we had to do was to put ourselves into the mental state of an idiot and write a ridiculous hill-billy tune. So we went to work with a will, vowing to make thousands by simply being simple-minded. We worked for an hour and then gave up in hysterical despair. Impossible. We found ourselves being "personal" and "expressing ourselves"; and try as we might we couldn't seem to boil any music down to the bare, feeble-minded level we had set ourselves. I remember that at one point we were trying like two children, one note at a time, to make a tune that didn't even require any harmony, it would be that obvious. Impossible. It was a revealing experiment, I must say, even though it left us with a slightly doomed feeling. As I say, why don't you tear up my contract?

(I drain the already empty coffee cup.)

P.M.

(With a touch of the basketball coach): Doom, nothing. I'll bet my next week's salary that you can write simple tunes if you really put your mind to it. And not with another composer, but all by yourself. After all, George was just like you, highbrow, one foot in Carnegie Hall and the other in Tin Pan Alley. He wrote concert music, too, and was all wound up in fancy harmony and counter-point and orchestration. He just knew when to be simple and when not to be.

L.B.

No, I think you're wrong. Gershwin was a whole other man. No connection at all.

P.M.

You're only being modest, or pretending to be. Didn't that critic after your last show call you a second Gershwin, or a budding Gershwin, or something?

L.B.

(Secretly flattered): That's all in the critic's mind. Nothing to do with facts. Actually Gershwin and I came from opposite sides of the tracks, and if we meet anywhere at all it's in my love for his music. But there it ends. Gershwin was a songwriter who grew into a serious composer. I am a serious composer trying to be a

songwriter. His was by far the more normal way: starting with small forms and blossoming out from there. My way is more confused: I wrote a symphony before I ever wrote a popular song. How can you expect me to have that simple touch that he had?

P.M.
(*Paternally*): But George—did you know him, by the way?

L.B.
I wish I had. He died when I was just a kid in Boston.

P.M.
(*A star in his eye*): If you had met him you would have known that George was every inch a serious composer. Why, look at the *Rhapsody in Blue,* the *American in—*

L.B.
Now, P.M., you know as well as I do that the *Rhapsody* is not a composition at all. It's a string of separate paragraphs stuck together— with a thin paste of flour and water. Composing is a very different thing from writing tunes, after all. I find that the themes, or tunes, or whatever you want to call them, in the *Rhapsody* are terrific— inspired, God-given. At least four of them, which is a lot for a twelve-minute piece. They are perfectly harmonized, ideally proportioned, songful, clear, rich, moving. The rhythms are always right. The "quality" is always there, just as it is in his best show tunes. But you can't just put four tunes together, God-given though they may be, and call them a composition. Composition means a putting together, yes, but a putting together of elements so that they add up to an organic whole. *Compono, componere—*

P.M.
Spare us the Latin. You can't mean that the *Rhapsody in Blue* is not an organic work! Why, in its every bar it breathes the same thing, throughout all its variety and all its change of mood and tempo. It breathes America— the people, the urban society that George knew deeply, the pace, the nostalgia, the nervousness, the majesty, the—

L.B.

— the Chaikovsky sequences, the Debussy meanderings, the Lisztian piano-fireworks. It's as American as you please while the themes are going on; but the minute a little thing called development is called for, America goes out the window and Chaikovsky and his friends march in the door. And the trouble is that a composition *lives* in its development.

P.M.

I think I need some more coffee. Waiter!

L.B.

Me too. I didn't mean to get started on all this, and I certainly don't want to tread on your idol's clay feet. He's my idol too, remember. I don't think there has been such an inspired melodist on this earth since Chaikovsky, if you want to know what I really feel. I rank him right up there with Schubert and the great ones. But if you want to speak of a *composer*, that's another matter. Your *Rhapsody in Blue* is not a real composition in the sense that whatever happens in it must seem inevitable, or even pretty inevitable. You can cut out parts of it without affecting the whole in any way except to make it shorter. You can remove any of these stuck-together sections, and the piece still goes on as bravely as before. You can even interchange these sections with one another, and no harm done. You can make cuts within a section, or add new cadenzas, or play it with any combination of instruments or on the piano alone; it can be a five-minute piece or a six-minute piece or a twelve-minute piece. And in fact all these things are being done to it every day. It's still the *Rhapsody in Blue*.

P.M.

But look here. That sounds to me like the biggest argument yet in its favor. If a piece is so sturdy that whatever you do to it has no effect on its intrinsic nature, then it must be pretty healthy. There must be something there that resists pressure, something real and alive, wouldn't you say?

L.B.

Of course there is: those tunes. Those beautiful tunes. But they still don't add up to a piece.

P.M.

Perhaps you're right in a way about the *Rhapsody*. It was an early work, after all— his first attempt to write in an extended form. He was only twenty-six or so, don't forget; he couldn't even orchestrate the piece when he wrote it. But how about the later works? What about the *American in Paris?* Now that is surely a well-knit, organic—

L.B.

True, what you say. Each work got better as he went on, because he was an intelligent man and a serious student, and he worked hard. But the *American in Paris* is again a study in tunes, all of them beautiful, and all of them separate. He had by that time discovered certain tricks of composition, ways of linking themes up, of combining and developing motives, of making an orchestral fabric. But even here they still remain tricks, mechanisms borrowed from Strauss and Ravel and who knows where else. And when you add it all up together it is still a weak work because none of these tricks is his own. They don't arise from the nature of the material; they are borrowed and applied to the material. Or rather *appliquéed* to it, like beads on a dress. When you hear the piece you rejoice in the first theme, then sit and wait through the "filler" until the next one comes along. In this way you sit out about two thirds of the composition. The remaining third is marvelous because it consists of the themes themselves; but where's the composition?

P.M.

(*A bit craftily*): But you play it all the time, don't you?

L.B.

Yes.

P.M.

And you've recorded it, haven't you?

L.B.

Yes.

P.M.

Then you must like it a lot, mustn't you?

L.B.

I adore it. Ah, here's the coffee.

P.M.

(*Sighing*): I don't understand you. How can you adore something you riddle with holes? Can you adore a bad composition?

L.B.

Each man kills the thing he loves. Yes, I guess you can love a bad composition. For non-compositional reasons. Sentiment. Association. Inner meaning. Spirit. But I think I like it most of all because it is so sincere. It is trying so hard to be good; it has only good intentions.

P.M.

You mean you like it for its faults?

L.B.

No, I don't. But what's good in it is so good that it's irresistible. If you have to go along with some chaff in order to have the wheat, it's worth it. And I love it because it shows, or begins to show, what Gershwin might have done if he had lived. Just look at the progress from the *Rhapsody* to the piano concerto, from the concerto to—

P.M.

(*Glowing*): Ah, the concerto is a masterpiece.

L.B.

That's your story. The concerto is the work of a young genius who is learning fast. But *Porgy and Bess*— there the real destiny of Gershwin begins to be clear.

P.M.

Really, I don't get it. Doesn't *Porgy* have all the same faults? I'm always being told that it's perhaps the weakest composition of all he wrote, in spite of the glorious melodies in it. He intended it as a grand opera, after all, and it seems to have failed as a grand opera. Whenever a production of *Porgy* really succeeds, you find that it's been changed into a sort of operetta. They have taken out all the "in-between" singing and replaced it with spoken lines, leaving only the main numbers. That seems to me to speak for itself.

L.B.

Oh, no. It speaks only for the producers. It's a funny thing about *Porgy:* I always miss the in-between singing when I hear it in its cut form. Perhaps it is more successful that way; it certainly is for the public. It may be because so much of that recitative seems alien to the character of the songs themselves, instead recalling *Tosca* and *Pelléas.* But there's a danger of throwing out the baby with the bath. Because there's a lot of that recitative that *is* in the character of the songs and fits the opera perfectly. Do you remember Bess's scene with Crown on the island? Bess is saying *(Singing):*

>"It's like dis, Crown,
>I's the only woman Porgy ever had—"

P.M.

(Joining in rapturously):

>"An I's thinkin' now,
>How it will be tonight
>When all these other niggers go back to
>   Catfish Row."

L.B. and P.M.

(Together, with growing excitement):

>"He'll be sittin' and watchin' the big front gate,
>A-countin' 'em off waitin' for Bess.
>An' when the last woman—"

(The restaurant is all eyes and ears.)

P.M.

(In a loud whisper): I think we are making a scene.

L.B.

(In a violent whisper): But that's just what I mean! Thrilling stuff, isn't it? Doesn't it point the way to a kind of Gershwin music that would have reached its own perfection eventually? I can never get over the horrid fact of his death for that reason. With *Porgy*

you suddenly realize that Gershwin was a great, great theater composer. He always had been. Perhaps that's what was wrong with his concert music: it was really theater music thrust into a concert hall. What he would have done in the theater in another ten or twenty years! And then he would still have been a young man! What a loss! Will America ever realize what a loss it was?

P.M.
(*Moved*): You haven't touched your coffee.

L.B.
(*Suddenly exhausted*): It's gotten cold. Anyway, I have to go home and write music. Thanks for lunch, P.M.

P.M.
Oh, thank you for coming. I've enjoyed it. Let's do it again, shall we? We have so much to talk about.

L.B.
(*With a glance at the skating rink*): Like what, for instance?

P.M.
Well, for one thing, that show of yours. Very strange. It's a big success, the public enjoys it, it's been running for five months, and there's not a hit in it. How do you explain it?

(APRIL 1955)

Interlude:

Upper Dubbing, Calif.

INTERLUDE:
UPPER DUBBING,
CALIF.

There is a place in California which does not appear on any map and is known as Upper Dubbing. No county seat, Upper Dubbing is simply a large room on the third floor of the Sound Department Building at Columbia Pictures' studios— a room where sound and image meet, are balanced and synchronized. More important, it is in this room that the various sound tracks which eventually compose the final sound-complex heard by millions in the movie houses are unified and adjusted— where the dialogue track, the music track, and the sound-effects track are, in other words, "dubbed" into the picture. Three quiet, dignified, brilliantly competent gentlemen sit at three sections of a huge desklike instrument that makes one think of a tribunal and manipulate an array of dials, switches and buttons that put to shame the equipment of a comic-strip mad scientist. The head man of these three wizards is Dick Olson, an authentic genius, and to be praised as much for his unaccountably even temper under outrageously trying circumstances as for his fine work. He and his side men are facing an enormous screen which fills all of the far wall and which is backed by huge amplifiers, stereophonic, monaural, binaural, and otherwise.

For Dick Olson and his magic I hold the awe-struck admiration I have often observed in literary folk when they see a composer at work. "How do you know just what dots and lines to put down on the ruled paper? How can you tell just how they're going to sound— that one cluster of dots can make me wince or thrill, or another one achieve an effect of glorious serenity?" The Olsons of the world practice a magic blacker and— to me, at least— more mysterious than that, and somehow do it to very specific and mutually conflicting orders. For instance, he may be told to keep the audience unconsciously aware of the traffic noise of a great city, yet they must also be aware of the sounds of wind and waves coming into a large, almost empty church *over* those traffic noises. And meantime the pedaling of a child's bicycle going around the church must punctuate the dialogue of two stray characters who have wandered in. Not a word of that dialogue, of course, must be lost, and the voices at the same time must arouse the dim echoes they would have in so cavernous a setting. And at this particular point no one (except the composer) has even begun to think how the musical background can fit in.

These apparently mutually self-defeating orders emanate from a row of armchairs behind Olson, occupied by the producer, the director, the composer, the chief editor, and the music cutters, all of whom presume to know everything about the picture to be dubbed, all of whom have conflicting notions of how to achieve the best results, all of whom have a compulsive desire to make these notions heard. Is Dick Olson sent promptly screaming to the nearest madhouse, as one might reasonably expect? No, he listens quietly and then calmly leans forward to that bewildering maze of dials, switches and buttons, twists, shoves and pushes a couple of dozen of them, and within three minutes the playback has mixed every conflicting item into a witch's brew that delivers precisely what every single armchair was demanding!

The picture in question is *On the Waterfront*, an Elia Kazan production produced by S. P. Eagle, directed by Mr. Kazan, and released by Columbia Pictures. (The foregoing is too much for me to explain: I. am only quoting from the titles, and I am only the composer of the background music.) When I was first shown a rough cut of the picture I thought it a masterpiece of direction; and Marlon Brando seemed to me to be giving the greatest performance I had ever seen him give, which is saying a good deal. I was swept by my enthusiasm into accepting the commission to write the score, although I had thereto resisted all such offers on the grounds that it is a musically unsatisfactory experience for a composer to write a score whose chief merit ought to be its unobtrusiveness. It has often been said that the best dramatic background music for a motion picture is that which is not heard. At least, not consciously heard. If it is heard, something is wrong: it is in the way; it is no longer background music. Little inducement indeed for a composer. But all such thoughts were drowned in the surge of excitement I felt upon first seeing this film. I heard music as I watched: that was enough. And the atmosphere of talent that this film gave off was exactly the atmosphere in which I love to work and collaborate. I have since then seen the picture some fifty times, in sections or *in toto,* and I have never changed in my re-action. Day after day I sat at a movieola, running the print back and forth, measuring in feet the sequences I had chosen for music, converting feet into seconds by mathematical formula, making homemade cue sheets; and every time I wept at the same speeches, chuckled at the same gestures. This continued right through the composing, orchestrating, and recording of the music. But in Upper Dubbing I wept not; neither did I chuckle. For Upper Dubbing means serious business.

I was fortunate to be admitted at all to these dubbing sessions; I am told that usually the composer's work is finished on the recording stage. (There is another Hollywood joke to the effect that the composer had better listen hard to the playbacks of his score on the recording stage, for he may never hear it again.) Having been admitted to the dubbing room, I could at least put up the semblance of a fight. By this time, I had become so in-volved in each detail of the score that it seemed to me perhaps the most important part of the picture. I had to keep reminding my-self that it is really the *least* important part, that a spoken line covered by music is a line lost, and by that much a loss to the pic-ture, while a bar of music completely obliterated by speech is only a bar of music lost and *not* necessarily a loss to the picture. Over and over again I repeated this little maxim to myself, like a good Coué disciple, as I found myself pleading for a beloved G-flat. Sometimes there would be a general decision to cut an entire piece of music out of the picture because it seemed to "generalize" the emotional quality of a scene, whereas the director wished the scene to be "particularized." Sometimes the music would be turned off completely for some seconds to allow a line to stand forth stark and bare— and then be turned on again. Sometimes the music, which had been planned as a composition with a beginning, middle and end, would be silenced seven bars before the end. This is, of course, frustrating and maddening for the composer. But even more frustrating and maddening things may happen. For example, there is, in *On the Waterfront,* a tender, hesitant love scene on the roof between the inarticulate hero and the inhibited heroine, surrounded by cooing pigeons. It was deliberately underwritten, and there are long, Kazan-like pauses between the lines— an ideal spot, it would seem, for the composer to take over. I suggested that here I should write love music that was shy at first and then, with growing, *Tristanish* intensity, come to a great climax which swamps the scene and screen, even drowning out the last prosaic bits of dialogue, which went something like this:

> *"Have a beer with me?"*
> *(Very long pause)*
> *"Uh-huh."*

The music here was to do the real storytelling, and Kazan and company agreed enthusiastically, deciding to do it this way before even one note was written. So it was written, so orchestrated, so recorded.

But then, in Upper Dubbing, Kazan decided he just couldn't give up that ineffably sacred grunt which Brando emits at the end: it was, he thought, perhaps the two most eloquent syllables the actor had delivered in the whole script. And what happened to the music? As it mounts to its great climax, as the theme goes higher and higher and brasses and percussion join in with the strings and woodwinds, the all-powerful control dials are turned, and the sound fades out in a slow *diminuendo.* Musically ridiculous, of course; and to save a grunt, the tension on the screen is lessened in precisely the proportion that it mounts in my own pummeled psyche. *Uh-huh.*

Such are the things sometimes done in Upper Dubbing; for it is impossible to know in advance how it will all work out when, for the first time, music, dialogue (including grunts), sound effects, and image all collide with a shattering roar in the dubbing room.

And so the composer sits by, protesting as he can, but ultimately accepting, be it with heavy heart, the inevitable loss of a good part of his score. Everyone tries to comfort him. "You can always use it in a suite." Cold comfort. It is for the good of the picture, he repeats numbly to himself; it is for the good of the picture.

And, after all is said and done, the others are right. The whole picture *is* what counts; and the composer must see it not as a composer but as a man of the theater. Then the gratifications are many: he sees how the score has helped to blend atmospheres, to provide continuity, or to add a dimension by telling an inner story not overtly articulated in the dialogue or·the action. For a score, judiciously applied to a film, can infuse it with a warm breath of its own, while one bar too many of music can be a serious detriment. But oh, the pain of losing that bar; and oh, the fight the composer will put up for it!

Through it all, Dick Olson and his adjutants sit quietly at their forest of dials, waiting patiently for the armchair generals behind them to come to some decision. Once, during a particularly stubborn deadlock, we found a softball and let off steam in a fifteen-minute session of catch— always taking care, of course, to avoid hitting Harry Cohn's $5,000 screen. Then, somehow, the decision was made.

(MAY 1954)

Photograph Section

Part of a demonstration of the differences between the early and final versions of Beethoven's *Fifth Symphony*. The score has been blown up to huge dimensions on the studio floor. *(page 85)*

All photographs copyright Roy Stevens

A production number in "American Musical Comedy":
Leonard Bernstein watches a scene from *Of Thee I Sing*.
(page 164)

An exploration of the structure of modern music, by means of a set of children's blocks. ("Introduction to Modern Music," *page 192*)

A blackboard demonstration of Bach's numerology. ("The Music of Johann Sebastian Bach," *page 237*)

The orchestra and the chorus under Leonard Bernstein
perform a passage from Bach's *St. Matthew's Passion*.
(page 237)

Photos taken
during the
telecast of the
*St. Matthew's
Passion.*
(page 237)

II

Seven Omnibus

Television Scripts

BEETHOVEN'S FIFTH SYMPHONY

TELECAST: NOVEMBER 14, 1954

Leonard Bernstein:

We are going to try to perform for you today a curious and rather difficult experiment. We're going to take the first movement of Beethoven's *Fifth Symphony* and rewrite it. Now don't get scared; we're going to use only notes that Beethoven himself wrote. We're going to take certain discarded sketches that Beethoven wrote, intending to use them in this symphony, and find out why he rejected them, by putting them back into the symphony and seeing how the symphony would have sounded with them. Then we can guess at the reason for rejecting these sketches, and, what is more important, perhaps we can get a glimpse into the composer's mind as it moves through this mysterious creative process we call composing.

(L. B. looks around at score)

We have here painted on the floor a reproduction of the first page of the conductor's score for Beethoven's *Fifth Symphony*. Every time I look at this orchestral score I am amazed all over again at its simplicity, strength and rightness. And how economical the music is! Why, almost every bar of this first movement is a direct development of these opening four notes:

85

And what are these notes that they should be so pregnant and meaningful that a whole symphonic movement can be born of them? Three G's and an E-flat. Nothing more. Anyone could have thought of them— maybe . . .

People have wondered for years what it is that endows this musical figure with such potency. All kinds of fanciful music-appreciation theories have been advanced: that it is based on the song of a bird Beethoven heard in the Vienna woods; that it is Fate knocking at the door; that it's the trumpets announcing the Judgment Day. And more of the same.

But none of these interpretations tells us anything. The truth is that the real meaning lies in all the notes that follow it, all the notes of all the five-hundred measures of music that follow it in this first movement. And Beethoven, more than any other composer before or after him, I think, had the ability to find exactly the right notes that had to follow his themes. But even he, with this great ability, had a gigantic struggle to achieve this rightness: not only the right notes, but the right rhythms, the right climaxes, the right harmonies, the right instrumentation. And it's that struggle that we would like to investigate.

Actually there are two struggles that every composer has. One is to find the right notes for themes; the other is to find the right notes to follow themes, to justify these themes as *symphonic* themes. We're all pretty familiar with the first of these struggles. We have all been privileged to watch Schumann and Brahms and other greats of the silver screen laboring over the keyboard as they search for the right tune. We have all seen Jimmy Cagney as George M. Cohan, dramatically alone on a bare stage with solitary work light, picking out the immortal notes of "Over There."

But spurious or not, the struggle is real. Beethoven, too, shared in that struggle in a very real way. We know from his notebooks that he wrote down at least fourteen versions of the melody that opens the *second* movement of this symphony. This is the way we know it today:

L. B. plays at piano:

Andante con moto

Fourteen versions over a period of eight years! Here is one of these versions, which is very different:

And here is another:

After eight years of experimenting with twelve others, he ultimately combined the most interesting and graceful elements of all versions and arrived at the tune which is familiar.

But now that he has his theme, the big struggle begins. Now comes the job of giving symphonic meaning to the theme, a meaning which becomes clear only after we have arrived at the very last note of the entire movement. Thus, returning to the first movement, the famous four notes:

are not in themselves susceptible of "meaning" in the music-appreciation sense. They are really a springboard for the symphonic continuity to come. That is the real function of what is called *form*. Form is not a mold for Jello, into which we pour notes and expect the result automatically to be a rondo, or a minuet, or a sonata. The real function of form is to take us on a varied and complicated half-hour journey of continuous symphonic progress. To do this, the composer must have his inner road map. He must have the ability to know what the next destination will be—in other words, what the next note has to be to convey a sense of *rightness*, a sense that whatever note succeeds the last is the only possible note that can happen at that precise instant. As we have said, Beethoven could do this better than anyone, but he also struggled with all his force in the doing. Let's try to follow this struggle.

To begin with, Beethoven chose to use twelve different instruments to make up his orchestra in his first movement:

(The twelve players take positions at indicated points of score painted on floor.)

The full orchestra, of course, is made up of these twelve instruments multiplied anywhere from two to eighteen times.

(The musicians slowly walk across the page of music)

As the conductor views this score, his eye has to follow all the instruments simultaneously across the page.

However, for his opening bars, Beethoven did not wish the entire orchestra to be playing. And so he dismissed five instruments: the oboe, bassoon, horn, trumpet and tympany. Here is the original manuscript as he started it, with the remaining seven instruments accounted for:

But note that there is again something crossed out, the part of the flute. So we know that Beethoven, for one second, *was* going to include the flute. Why did he cross it out? Simply because the high, piping notes of the flute don't seem to fit into the generally rude and brusque atmosphere of the opening bars. Beethoven clearly wanted these notes to be a strong, masculine utterance, and he therefore orchestrated entirely with instruments that play normally in the register of the male singing voice.

(Orchestra plays first with the flute, then without it)

The flute, being the instrumental equivalent of a soprano, would
be intruding here like a delicate lady at a club smoker. So out
came the flute.

You see, a lot of us assume, when we hear the symphony today,
that it must have spilled out of Beethoven in one steady gush,
clear and right from the beginning. But not at all. Beethoven left
pages and pages of discarded material, similar to these, in his own
writing, enough to fill a sizable book. The man rejected, rewrote,
scratched out, tore up, and sometimes altered a passage as many
as twenty times. We can see some of these alterations in this fac-
simile of the original orchestral manuscript score:

L. B. looks at original score:

Look at those agonized changes, those feverish scrawls.

Here is a passage:

that has been corrected so many times that there is no longer room for the final version. So he had to put that in as a footnote at the bottom of the page, and left it up to his copyists to figure out what he really meant.

I admire and pity those copyists.

Now for contrast, look at one of Stravinsky's scores: how neat, how unagonized. It looks almost as beautiful as it sounds:

But Beethoven's manuscript looks like a bloody record of a tremendous inner battle. Before he began to write this wild-looking score, he had for three years been filling notebooks with sketches. We have some of them here, some that he ultimately discarded as not right. I have been trying to figure out what his first movement would have sounded like if he had left some of these sketches in. I have been experimenting with the music, speculating on where these sketches might have been intended for use, and putting them back in those places to see what the piece might have been had he used them, and I have come up with some curious and interesting results. Let's see what they are.

We already know too well the opening bars of this symphony:

Now once Beethoven had made this initial statement, what then? How does he go on to develop it? He does it like this:

But here is a discarded sketch which is also a direct and immediate development of those same four notes:

Not very good, and not very bad, taken all by itself. But it is a
good, logical development of the opening figure. What would the
music sound like if Beethoven had used this sketch as the immediate development of his theme? We can find out by simply putting the sketch back into the symphony, and it will sound like this:

Orchestra:

It does make a difference, doesn't it? Not only because it sounds wrong to our ears, which are accustomed to the version we know, but also because of the nature of the music itself. It is so symmetrical that it seems static. The left hand imitates the right hand in monkeylike fashion. It doesn't seem to want to go anywhere, and that is fatal at the outset, especially of a symphonic journey. It doesn't seem to have the mystery about it that the right version has, or that whispering promise of things to come. It gets stuck in its own repetitions and doesn't "build." And Beethoven was first and foremost a builder.

Let us look at another rejected sketch. Here is one that sounds like this (again it is based, as all of them are, on that same opening figure):

Piano:

Now my guess is that he would have used it somewhere in this passage:

Orchestra:

Now the same passage with discarded sketch included:

Orchestra:

Terrible, isn't it? This sketch just intrudes itself into the living flow of the music and stands there, repeating, grounded, until such time as the music can take off in its flight. No wonder Beethoven rejected it! For he, of all people, had a sense of drive through his music that is second to none. But this sketch just doesn't arrive. It is again, like the first, static and stuck.

Now *this* sketch is different. It has real excitement and "build":

Piano:

I suspect it was intended for a spot a little later on in the movement— here:

Orchestra:

col 8va bassa

This is certainly one of the most climactic and thrilling moments in the movement. It is the beginning of the coda, or the last big push before the end. Let's see how it would have sounded using the sketch I just played you:

Orchestra:

col 8va bassa - - - -

Not at all bad. It has logic, and it builds. But the version that Beethoven finally did use has so much more logic, and builds with so much more ferocity and shock, that there is no comparison:

Piano:

col 8va bassa

The other, although good, seems pale beside it.

Now here is a sketch that I really like, because it sounds like the essential Beethoven style. It reminds me a bit of the *Pathetique Sonata:*

Piano:

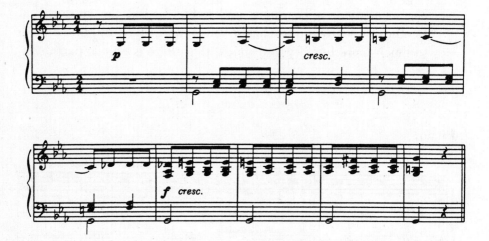

This sketch has pain in it, and mystery, and a sense of eruption. It would have fitted very neatly into the coda— harmonically, rhythmically, and every other way except emotionally. Here is the spot in the coda I mean:

Orchestra:

Now let us add the sketch to it:

Orchestra:

Do you hear the difference? What has happened? We had to come down from a high point to a low point in order to build up again dramatically to a still higher point. This is, in itself, good and acceptable dramatic structure. It happens all the time in plays and novels as well as in music. But this is no moment for it. Beethoven has already reached his high point; he is already in the last lap; and he wants to smash forward on that high level right to the end. And he does with astonishing brilliance. It is this genius for going forward, always forward, that in every case guides his hand in the struggle with his material. Why, even the very ending was written three different ways on this orchestral score. Here is the first ending he wrote— an abrupt, typically Beethovenian ending:

Orchestra:

Why did he reject it? It seems perfectly all right and satisfying. But no, he apparently felt that it was too abrupt; and so he went right on and wrote a second ending that was more extended, more like a finale, more noble, romantic, majestic. It went like this:

Orchestra:

But, as you can see in the manuscript, this ending is also buried beneath the crossing-out. Now he felt it was too long, too pretentious, too majestic. It didn't seem to fit into the scheme of the whole movement, where the main quality is a bare, pithy, economical, forthright, direct statement of the greatest possible force. And so he tried still a third ending, and this one worked. But the odd thing is that, as it turned out, the third ending is even more abrupt than the first! So you see, he had to struggle and agonize before he realized so apparently simple a thing: that the trouble with his first ending was not that it was too short, but that it was not short enough. Thus he arrived at the third ending, which is as right as rain. This is how we hear it today:

Orchestra:

And so Beethoven came to the end of his symphonic journey, for one movement, that is. Imagine a whole lifetime of this struggle, movement after movement, symphony after symphony, sonata after quartet after concerto. Always probing and rejecting in his dedication to perfection, to the principle of *inevitability*. This somehow is the key to the mystery of a great artist: that for reasons unknown to him or to anyone else, he will give away his energies and his life just to make sure that one note follows another inevitably. It seems rather an odd way to spend one's life; but it isn't so odd when we think that the composer, by doing this, leaves us at the finish with the feeling that something is right in the world, that something checks throughout, something that follows its own laws consistently, something we can trust, that will never let us down.*

(The telecast concluded with a performance of the first movement of Beethoven's Fifth Symphony.)

* The last sentence was borrowed from "Why Beethoven?," page 21.

TELECAST: OCTOBER 16, 1955

Jazz band:

Leonard Bernstein:

Now, anyone hearing this music, anyone on any civilized part of this earth, east or west, pole to pole, would immediately say: That is jazz. We are going to try to investigate jazz, not through the usual historical approach which has become all too familiar, but through approaching the music itself. We are going to examine the musical "innards" of jazz to find out once and for all what it is that sets it apart from all other music.

Jazz is a very big word; it covers a multitude of sounds, all the way from the earliest Blues to Dixieland bands, to Charleston bands, to Swing bands, to Boogie-Woogie, to crazy Bop, to cool Bop, to Mambo—and much more. It is all jazz, and I love it because it is an original kind of emotional expression, in that it is never wholly sad or wholly happy. Even the Blues has a robustness and hard-boiled quality that never lets it become sticky-sentimental, no matter how self-pitying the words are.

Blues singer:

"EMPTY BED BLUES"
by J. C. Johnson

Slowly

aw - ful a- chin' head _____ My

new man had left me just a room and a emp - ty

bed _____

And, on the other hand, the gayest, wildest jazz always seems to have some hint of pain in it. Listen to this trumpet, and see what I mean:

Trumpet:

"OLE MISS"
by W. C. Handy

That is what intrigues me about jazz; it is unique, a form of expression all its own.

I love it also for its humor. It really plays with notes. We always speak of "playing" music: we play Brahms or we play Bach— a term perhaps more properly applied to tennis. But jazz is real play. It "fools around" with notes, so to speak, and has fun with them. It is, therefore, entertainment in the truest sense.

But I find I have to defend jazz to those who say it is low-class. As a matter of fact, all music has low-class origins, since it comes from folk music, which is necessarily earthy. After all, Haydn minuets are only a refinement of simple, rustic German dances, and so are Beethoven scherzos. An aria from a Verdi opera can often be traced back to the simplest Neapolitan fisherman. Besides, there has always been a certain shadow of indignity around music, particularly around the players of music.

I suppose it is due to the fact that historically *players* of music seem to lack the dignity of *composers* of music. But this is especially true of jazz, which is almost completely a player's art, depending as it does on improvisation rather than on composition. But this also means that the player of jazz is himself the real composer, which gives him a creative, and therefore *more* dignified, status.

Then there are those who argue that jazz is loud. But so are Sousa marches, and we don't hear complaints about them. Besides, it's not always loud. It is very often extremely delicate, in fact. Perhaps this objection stems from the irremediable situation of what is after all a kind of brass band playing in a room too small for it. But that is not the fault of jazz itself.

However, the main argument against jazz has always been that it is not art. I think it *is* art, and a very special art. And before we can argue about whether it is or not, we must know *what* it is; and so I propose to share with you some of the things I know and love about jazz.

Let's take that Blues we heard before and find out what it's made of:

Jazz band:

Now what are the elements that make that jazz?

First of all there is the element of melody. Western music in general is based, melodically speaking, on scales, like the major scale you all practiced as kids:

L. B. plays piano:

But there is a special one for jazz, which is a variation of that regular major scale.

In jazz, this scale gets modified three different times. The third note gets lowered from this:

to this:

The fifth from this:

to this:

And the seventh from this:

to this:

Those three changed notes are called "blue notes."

(Major scale with blue notes) *

♭3   ♭5   ♭7
blue   *blue*   *blue*

* Actually, these blue notes are most commonly used in terms of the descending scale:

So instead of a phrase which would ordinarily go something like
this:

which is not particularly jazzy— we would get, using blue notes,
this phrase:

— which begins to show a jazz quality.

But this so-called "jazz scale" is used only melodically. In the
harmony underneath we still use our old unflatted notes, and that
causes dissonances to happen between that tune and the chords:

L. B. plays piano:

But these very dissonances have a true jazz sound. For example,
jazz pianists are always using these two dissonant notes together:

— and there is a reason for it. They are really searching for a note that isn't there at all, but one which lies somewhere between the two notes— between this:

and this:

and the note is called a quarter-tone.

The quarter-tone comes straight from Africa, which is the cradle of jazz and where quarter-tones are everyday stuff. We can produce one on a wind instrument or a stringed instrument or with the voice, but on the piano we have to approximate it by playing together the two notes on each side of it:

The real note is somewhere in there, in that crack between them.

Let's see if I can sing you that quarter-tone, if you will forgive my horrid voice. Here is an African Swahili tune I once heard. The last note of it is a quarter-tone:

L. B. sings:

quarter tones

Sounds as if I'm singing terribly out of tune, but actually I am singing a real note in another musical language. In jazz it is right at home.

L. B. plays piano:

Now, just to show you how important these so-called "blue notes" are to jazz, let's hear that same Blues played without them, using only the plain white notes of the scale:

Clarinet:

There is something missing, isn't there? It just isn't jazz.

But even more important than melody in jazz is the element of rhythm. Rhythm is the first thing you associate with the word *jazz*, after all. There are two aspects to this point. The first is the beat. This is what you hear when the drummer's foot is beating the drum:

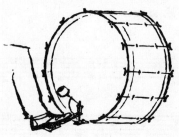

or when the bass player is plucking his bass:

or even when the pianist is kicking the pedal with his foot:

All this is elementary. The beats go on from beginning to end of a number, two or four of them to a measure, never changing in tempo or in meter. This is the heartbeat, so to speak, of jazz.

But more involved, and more interesting, is the rhythm going on *over* the beat— rhythmic figures which depend on something called "syncopation," a word you have certainly heard but maybe were never quite sure of. A good way to understand syncopation might be to think of a heartbeat that goes along steadily and, at a moment of shock, misses a beat. It is that much of a physical reaction.

Technically, syncopation means either the removal of an accent where you expect one, or the placing of an accent where you least expect one. In either case, there is the element of surprise and shock. The body responds to this shock, either by compensating for the missing accent or by reacting to the unexpected one.

Now where do we expect accents? Always on the first beat of a bar, on the downbeat. If there are two beats in a bar, *one* is going to be strong, *two* is going to be weak— exactly as in marching: *right*, left, *right*, left. Even if there are four beats in a bar, it is still like marching. Although we all have only two legs, the sergeant still counts out in four: *hup*, 2, 3, 4, *hup*, 2, 3, 4. There is always that natural accent on *one*. Take it away, and there is a simple syncopation:

L. B. gasps during missing first beat:

$$(\,!\,)\; 2, 3, 4 \qquad (\,!\,)\; 2, 3, 4 \;\text{ETC.}$$

You see that that missing accent on the first beat evokes a body response.

Now, the other way to make syncopation is exactly the reverse: put an accent on a weak beat, the second or the fourth, where it doesn't belong. Like this:

One, *TWO*, three, *FOUR*
One, *TWO*, three, *FOUR*

This is what we all do, listening to jazz, when we clap our hands or snap our fingers on the offbeat.

Those are the basic facts of syncopation; and now we can understand its subtler aspects. Between one beat and another there lie shorter and even weaker beats; and when these get accents the shock is correspondingly greater, since the weaker the beat you accentuate, the greater the surprise. Let's take eight of those fast beats in a bar: 1 2 3 4 5 6 7 8. The normal accents would fall on one and five: 1! 2 3 4 5! 6 7 8. Now, instead, let's put a big accent on a real weak one, the fourth:

$$1\; 2\; 3\; 4!\; 5\; 6\; 7\; 8$$

(Drum takes up from count, then claves, trumpet, etc.)

pizz.

As you see, we get a pure rhumba rhythm.

Of course, the strongest syncopation of all would obviously be obtained by doing both things at once: putting an accent on a weak beat and taking away the accent from the strong. So now we will do this double operation: put a wallop on the weak fourth, and remove the strong fifth beat entirely; and we get:

1 2 3 4!   — 6 7 8

(Various percussion instruments take it up)

It begins to sound like the Congo, doesn't it?

Trumpet adds melody:

Now that you've heard what syncopation is like, let's see what that same Blues we heard before would sound like without it. I think you'll miss that essential element, the very life of jazz:

Played "square" by sax, no vibrato:

Sounds "square," doesn't it?

Well, that takes care of two very important elements: melody and rhythm. But jazz could not be jazz without its special tonal colors, the actual sound values you hear. These colors are many, but they mostly stem from the quality of the Negro singing voice. For instance, when Louis Armstrong plays his trumpet, he is only doing another version of his own voice. Listen to an Armstrong record, like "I Can't Give You Anything but Love," and compare the trumpet solo with the vocal solo. You can't miss the fact that they're by the same fellow. But the Negro voice has engendered other imitations. The saxophone is in itself a kind of imitation of it— breathy, a little hoarse, with a vibrato, or tremor, in it.

(Here a saxophone plays a passage first with and then without vibrato)

Then there are all the different growls and rasps we get by putting mutes on the horns. Here, for example, is a trumpet with a cup mute:

(The sounds of these instruments are heard while they are being shown)

and a wah-wah mute:

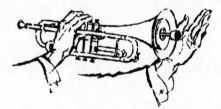

And a trombone with a plunger mute:

There are other tonal colors that derive from Afro-Cuban sources:
Bongo drums:

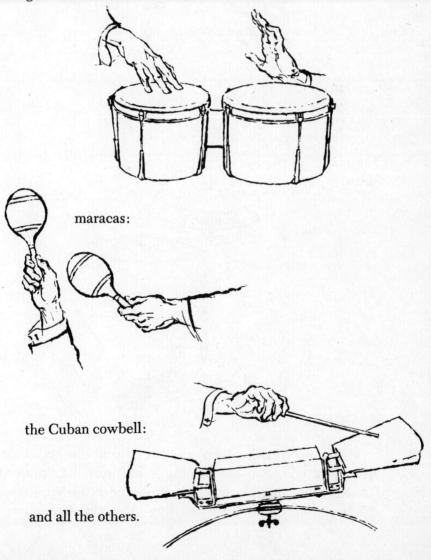

maracas:

the Cuban cowbell:

and all the others.

Then there are the colors that have an Oriental flavor:
the vibraphone:

the various cymbals:

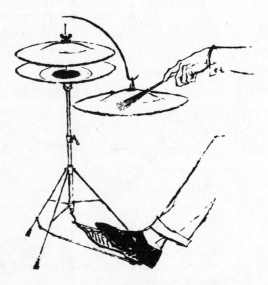

and so on.

These special colorations make their contribution to the total quality of jazz. You have certainly all heard jazz tunes played "straight" by non-jazz orchestras and wondered what was missing. There certainly is something missing— the coloration.

There is one more jazz element which may surprise some of you who think jazz is not an art. I refer to form. Did you know, for example, that the Blues is a classical form? Most people use the word *Blues* to mean any song that is "blue" or torchy or low-down or breast-beating— like "Stormy Weather," for example. But "Stormy Weather" is not a Blues, and neither is "Moanin' Low," nor "The Man I Love," or even "The Birth of the Blues." They are all popular songs.

The Blues is basically a strict poetic form combined with music. It is based on a rhymed couplet, with the first line repeated. For example, Billie Holiday sings:

> *"My man don't love me, treats me awful mean;*
> *Oh, he's the lowest man I've ever seen."*

But when she sings it, she repeats the first line— so it goes:

> *"My man don't love me, treats me awful mean;*
> *I said, my man don't love me, treats me awful mean;*
> *Oh, he's the lowest man I've ever seen."*

That is one stanza of Blues. A full Blues is nothing more than a succession of such stanzas for as long as the singer wishes.

Did you notice that the Blues couplet is, of all things, in iambic pentameter?

$$\smile \; - \; \smile \; - \; \smile \; - \; \smile \; - \; \smile \; -$$
> *"My man/don't love/me, treats/me aw/ful mean"*

This is about as classic as one can get. It means that you can take any rhymed couplet in iambic pentameter— from Shakespeare, for example— and make a perfect *Macbeth* Blues:

> *"I will not be afraid of death and bane,*
> *Till Birnam forest come to Dunsinane."*

It makes a lovely Blues:

L. B. sings:

Now if you've noticed, each of these three lines got four bars apiece, making it all a twelve-bar stanza. But the voice itself sang only about half of each four-bar line, and the rest is supposed to be filled up by the accompaniment. This filling-up is called a "break." And here in the break we have the origin of the instrument imitating the voice, the very soil in which jazz grows. Perhaps the essential sound of jazz is Louis Armstrong improvising the breaks in a Blues sung by Bessie Smith. From this kind of voice imitation all instrumental improvising has since developed.

Did you notice the instrument that has been accompanying our singers today? It is a harmonium, that wheezy little excuse for an organ which we all associate with hymn tunes. But far from being out of place in the Blues, this instrument is especially appropriate, since the chords in the Blues must always be exactly the same three chords we all know from hymn tunes:

L. B. plays on harmonium:

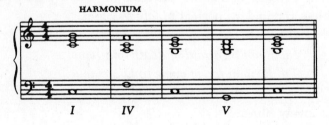

These chords must always remain in a strict classical pattern, pure and simple. Try to vary them, and the Blues quality flies out the window.

Well, there you have it: melody, rhythm, tone color, form, harmony. In each department there are special features that make *jazz*, instead of just music. Let's now put them all together, and hear a full-blown, all-out happy Blues. Oh, did you know that Blues could be happy? Just listen.

(Jazz Band plays a Blues arrangement of "King Porter Stomp," Dixieland style)

By this time I've probably given you the impression that jazz is nothing but Blues. Not at all. I've used the Blues to investigate jazz only because it embodies the various elements of jazz in so clear and pure a way. But the rest of jazz is concerned with applying these same elements to something called the popular song. The popular song, too, is a form; and it has certain strict patterns. Popular songs are in either two-part or three-part form. By far the most numerous are in the three-part. You all know this form, of course, from hearing it so much. It is as simple as pie. Anyone can write one.

Take "Sweet Sue," for instance. All you need is the first eight bars, really— which in the trade are called the front strain:

L. B. plays piano:

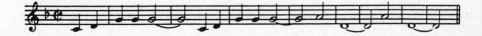

Now the song is practically written, since the whole thing will be only thirty-two bars long— four groups of eight bars apiece. The second eight is the same exactly as the first:

Sixteen bars, and we're already half finished. Now the next eight bars, which are called the release, or bridge, or just simply "the middle part," must be different music. But it doesn't matter if it's very good or not, since most people don't remember it too well anyway:

And then the same old front strain all over again:

and it's finished. Thirty-two bars, and a classic forever. Easy, isn't it?

But "Sweet Sue" is still not jazz. A popular song doesn't become jazz until it is improvised on, and there you have the real core of all jazz: improvisation. Remember, I said that jazz was a player's art rather than a composer's. Well, this is the key to the whole problem. It is the player who, by improvising, makes jazz. He uses the popular song as a kind of dummy to hang his notes on. He dresses it up in his own way, and it comes out an original. So the pop tune, in acquiring a new dress, changes its personality completely, like many people who behave one way in blue jeans and a wholly different way in dinner clothes. Some of you may object to this dressing-up. You say, "Let me hear the melody, not all this embroidery." But until you accept this principal of improvisation, you will never accept or understand jazz itself.

What does improvising mean? It means that you take a tune, keep it in mind with its harmony and all, and then, as they used to say, just "go to town," or make it up as you go along. You go to town by adding ornaments and figurations, or by making real old-fashioned variations just as Mozart and Beethoven did. Let me show you a little of how Mozart did it, and then you may understand how Erroll Garner does it. Mozart took a well-known nursery rhyme, which he knew as *"Ah, Vous Dirai-je Maman,"* and which we know as "Twinkle, Twinkle Little Star" or as a way of singing the alphabet:

L. B. plays piano and sings:

Now Mozart makes a series of variations. One of them begins:

Then another:

Another:

Andante

And another:

Allegro

They are all different pieces, yet they are all in one way or another that same original tune.

The jazz musician does exactly the same thing. There are infinite possible versions of "Sweet Sue," for example. The clarinet might improvise one chorus of it this way:

Clarinet:

Now he could have done that in any number of ways; and if I asked him to do it again tomorrow morning, it would come out a whole other piece. But it would still be "Sweet Sue," and it would still be jazz.

Now we come to the most exciting part of jazz, for me at any rate: simultaneous improvising. This happens when two or more musicians improvise on the same tune at the same time. Neither one knows exactly what the other is going to do; but they listen to each other, and pick up phrases from each other, and sort of talk together. What ties them together is the chords, the harmony, of "Sweet Sue." Over this harmony, they play two different melodic lines at the same time, which, in musical terms, makes a kind of accidental counterpoint. This is the germ of what is called the "jam session." Now the trumpet is going to join with the clarinet in a double improvisation on "Sweet Sue." See if you can distinguish the two melodic lines:

Trumpet and clarinet:

You see how exciting this can be? This business of improvising together gave rise to the style called Dixieland, which is constantly having a big revival. One of the most exhilarating sounds in all music is that of a Dixieland band blaring out its final chorus, all stops out, with everyone improvising together.

But jazz is not all improvization, not by a long shot. Much of it gets written down, and then it is called an arrangement. The great days of the arrangements were the Thirties, when big, startling swing arrangements were showing off the virtuosity of the great bands— like Casa Loma, Benny Goodman, Artie Shaw, the Dorsey brothers, and so on. Now jazz is hard to write down. There is no way of notating exactly those quarter-tones we talked about, nor the various smears and growls and subtle intonations. Even the rhythms can only be approximated in notation, so that much of the jazz quality is left to the instincts of the player who is reading the music. Still, it does work, because the instincts of these players are so deep and genuine.

Let's listen to a good, solid swing arrangement of a chorus of "Sweet Sue" as we might have heard it back in 1938.

Now remember, this arrangement was for dancing. In 1938 we were all dancing; and that brings up the most important point of all. Nobody seems to dance to jazz very much any more, except for mambo lovers, and they are limited to those who are athletic enough to do it. What has happened to dancing? We used to have a new dance practically every month: the Lindy Hop, the Shag, the Peabody, the Big Apple, Boogie, Susie-Q. Now we have only dances you have to take lessons to do.

What does this mean? Simply that the emphasis is on listening, these days, instead of on singing and dancing. This change had to happen. For one thing, the tremendous development of the recording industry has taught us to listen in a way we never did before. But even more significant, with the advent of more complicated swing and jazz like Boogie-Woogie and Bop, our interest has shifted to the music itself and to the virtuosity of its performance. That is, we are interested in what notes are being played, how well, how fast, and with what originality. You can't listen to Bop intelligently and dance too, murmuring sweet nothings into your partner's ear. You have to listen as hard as you can to hear what's happening.

So in a way, jazz has begun to be a kind of chamber music, an advanced sophisticated art mainly for listening, full of influences of Bartók and Stravinsky, and very, very serious. Let's listen for a moment to this kind of arrangement of our old friend "Sweet Sue."

Band plays very cool arrangement of "Sweet Sue":

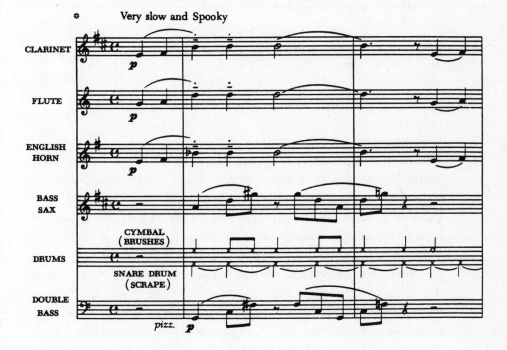

* Arrangement by Danny Hurd; reproduced by special permission.

Whether you call this kind of weird piece "cool" or "crazy" or "futuristic" or "modernistic" or whatever, the fact is that it is bordering on serious concert music. The arrangement begins to be a *composition*. Take away the beat, and you might not even know it's jazz at all. It would be just a concert piece. And why is it jazz? Because it is played by jazz men, on jazz instruments, and because it has its roots in the soil of jazz and not of Bach.

I think the key word to all this is the word *cool*. It means what it implies. Jazz used to advertise itself as "hot"; now the heat is off. The jazz player has become a highly serious person. He may even be an intellectual. He tends to wear Ivy League clothes, have a crew cut, or wear horn-rimmed glasses. He may have studied music at a conservatory or a university. This was unthinkable in the old days. Our new jazz man plays more quietly, with greater concentration on musical values, on tone quality, technique. He knows Bartók and Stravinsky, and his music shows it. He tends to avoid big, flashy endings. The music just stops when it is over.

As he has become cool, so have his listeners. They don't dance; they listen respectfully, as if to chamber music, and applaud politely at the end. At jazz night clubs all over the world you find audiences who do not necessarily have a drink in their hands and who do not beat out the rhythm and carry on as we did when I was a boy. It is all rather cool and surprisingly controlled, considering that jazz is essentially an emotional experience.

Where does this lead us in our investigation? To some pretty startling conclusions. There are those who conclude from all this that here, in the new jazz, is the real beginning of serious American music, that at last the American composer has his own expression. Of course when they say this they are intimating that all American symphonic works up to now are nothing but personalized imitations of the European symphonic tradition from Mozart to Mahler. Sometimes, I must say, I think they have a point. At any rate, we can be sure of one thing: that the line between serious music and jazz grows less and less clear. We have serious composers writing in the jazz idiom, and we have jazz musicians becoming serious composers. Perhaps we've stumbled on a theory.

But theory or no theory, jazz goes on finding new paths, sometimes reviving old styles, but, in either case, looking for freshness. In any art that is really vital and searching, splits are bound to develop; arguments arise and factions form. Just as in painting the non-objectivists are at sword's point with the representationalists, and in poetry the imagists declaim against the surrealists, so in jazz music we have a major battle between the traditionalists and the progressives.

These latter are the ones who are trying hardest to get away from the patterns of half a century, experimenting with new sonorities, using note relationships that are not common to the old jazz, and, in general, trying to keep jazz alive and interesting by broadening its scope. Jazz is a fresh, vital art in the present tense, with a solid past and an exciting future.

TELECAST: DECEMBER 4, 1955

(L. B. conducts first few bars of Brahms's First Symphony, *first movement. After first few bars he stops conducting, walks off podium, away from orchestra to center. Orchestra continues.)*

Leonard Bernstein:

You see, they don't need me. They do perfectly well by themselves.

The orchestra breaks down:

Well, maybe not *perfectly* well. People are constantly asking me: why is a conductor necessary? What does he do? Why does he carry on so? Isn't the orchestra after all a group of highly trained professional musicians? Don't they know how to count? Can't they read notes? Why do they need a fellow beating time for them? And if they do, what's so glamorous about beating time? Can't anybody do it? How about the concertmaster, the principal violin? Can't he indicate the movement of the piece with his bow? Well, as a matter of fact, he used to. There was an era of the so-called violin-conductor, whose main duty was to start and stop the orchestra and generally keep the flow of the music going. This was all well and good as long as orchestras were small enough. But around Beethoven's time, orchestras began getting larger and larger, and it soon became apparent that somebody had to be up there to keep the players together. So conducting as we know it is actually less than 150 years old.

The first real conductor in our sense of the word was Mendelssohn, who founded a tradition of conducting based on the concept of precision, as symbolized in the wooden stick we call the baton. Mendelssohn dedicated himself to an exact realization of the score he was conducting, through manipulation of that baton. There soon arrived, however, a great dissenter named Richard Wagner who declared that everything Mendelssohn was doing was wrong and that any conductor worth his salt should personalize the score he was conducting by coloring it with his own emotions and his own creative impulse. And so out of the clash of these two points of view the history of conducting was born; and there arose all those great names in conducting, as well as all the fights that go on about them right up to our own time. Mendelssohn fathered the "elegant"school, whereas Wagner inspired the "passionate" school of conducting. Actually, both attitudes are necessary, the Apollonian and the Dionysian, and neither one is completely satisfactory without the other. Both of them can be badly abused, as we know from having heard performances that seemed clear but were dry as dust, and others in which passion became simple distortion.

The ideal modern conductor is a synthesis of the two attitudes, and this synthesis is rarely achieved. In fact, it's practically impossible. Almost any musician can be a conductor, even a pretty good one; but only a rare musician can be a great one. This is not only because it is so hard to achieve the Mendelssohn–Wagner combination, but also because the conductor's work encompasses such a tremendous range. Unlike an instrumentalist or a singer, he has to play on an orchestra. His instrument is one hundred human instruments, each one a thorough musician, each with a will of his own; and he must cause them to play like one instrument with a single will. Therefore, he must have enormous authority, to say nothing of psychological insight in dealing with this large group— and all this is just the beginning. He must be a master of the mechanics of conducting. He must have an inconceivable amount of knowledge. He must have a profound perception of the inner meanings of music, and he must have uncanny powers of communication. If he has all this, he is the ideal conductor; and today we are going to try to find out once and for all what his functions really are.

Let's start with the mechanics and save the subtler details for later. The very first mechanical thing a conductor must master is the beat. Beating time is easy, relatively. Anyone can do it. You can do it. In fact, I'll show you how.

All you have to know is that music exists in time, and that time is divided up into measures or bars, and that each measure is further divided into equal subdivisions called beats, which go at a certain rate of speed. Now these bars can contain any number of beats from one on up, but the main thing is to know how to beat one, two, three or four beats per bar, since any number of beats above four per bar can be broken down into combinations of one, two, three and four. Now the first beat of any bar is always down:

L. B. picks up baton:

and the last beat of any bar is always up.

That is the first axiom of conducting. So if there is only one beat in a bar, it is both the first *and* last beat at the same time, and must therefore be down and immediately up again (so that you can be ready to come down again for the next bar), like this:

You see how easy it is.

Now, let's conduct a bit of music that goes in one beat to the bar— let's say, "The Skaters' Waltz." You all know how it goes.

L. B. sings, beating at the same time:

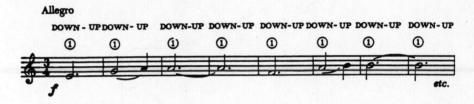

Now we are ready to conduct a full symphony orchestra in "The Skaters' Waltz." Here goes.

(L. B. gives four beats for nothing, sneakily cueing the orchestra in. They play thirty-two bars.)

That wasn't hard, was it? Are you surprised to find that a waltz goes in *one?* The popular belief is that a waltz is in three: one - two - three, one - two - three.

L. B. sings "Skaters' Waltz," beating three:

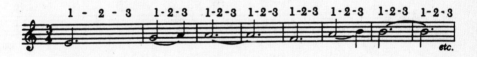

Well, it is. But the three beats are so fast that if one were to conduct them all, one would be beating endless numbers of tiny beats to no avail. Besides, it's exhausting and less clear to the orchestra. So instead we combine each group of three beats into one, which means that we beat only the first of the three and thus save ourselves from an early grave.

Now, with our acquired knowledge about beating one, let's try beating two. Remember that we said the first beat of any bar is down and the last beat must be up. Therefore it stands to reason that in order to beat two in a bar, we simply beat *one* down and *two* up, thus:

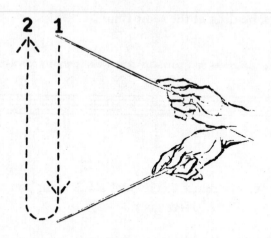

Now we're ready to conduct Beethoven's *Ninth*. Shall we try?

Orchestra:

We're making progress. The next thing to master is beating three. Here the only element we don't know about is the second beat. But we do know that the first beat is down and the third beat, being the last one, is up. The in-between beat, the second, is simply out to the side, away from the body— thus:

All three beats together would look like this:

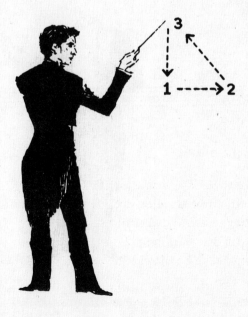

Shall we have a go at Schubert's *Unfinished Symphony?*

Orchestra:

All we have left to learn now is the beating of four. As we know, one is down and four is up. Two this time will be in toward the body:

and three will be out, away from the body:

so that the whole thing goes like this:

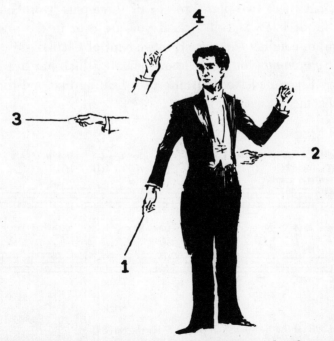

* *Note:* In practice a conductor seldom beats so squarely. The motion can, in fact, go to the other extreme of being very curvaceous.

Good. Let's beat some piece of music that goes in four— like the main theme from *Peter and the Wolf* by Prokofieff.

Orchestra:

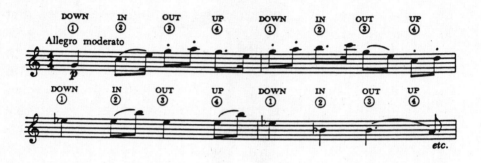

Well, now that we have conducted Beethoven's *Ninth*, Schubert's *Unfinished Symphony* and *Peter and the Wolf*, we are ready to conduct almost anything. For instance, if we are confronted by a piece which has *five* beats to a bar, we simply subdivide it into a combination of two-plus-three or of three-plus-two. Thus: 1 - 2, 1 - 2 - 3, or 1 - 2 - 3, 1 - 2.* So if you are ever in the position of having to conduct the second movement of Chaikovsky's *Pathét-ique Symphony* (you never know when!), which has five beats to a bar, all you have to do is alternate beating two and three, and you'll come out beating five.

*See page 126 for the two-beat and page 127 for the three-beat.

Having conducted all these great pieces, we can safely say we have *conducted* nothing at all. We have only been beating, and there's an eternity of difference between the two. Let's see what that difference is.

O.K. The conductor knows how to beat, but how and where does he practice? A violinist has a violin and practices on it at home; likewise for a piccolo or tuba player. But a conductor needs an instrument which is far too expensive to buy, far too large to house, and far too busy to be at his constant disposition. It is a real problem for a young conductor. He usually has to practice on thin air, by himself, perhaps in front of a mirror, perhaps following a phonograph record, but rarely with an orchestra following *him*.

Let us assume, however, that he *has* mastered the art of beating. He is still at the very beginning of the road to becoming a conductor. The plain truth is that beating business must do more than just count out the music for the orchestra. It must also convey the character of the music. There is an old-wives tale which says that the right hand should simply beat time, while the left hand is in charge of expressing emotion. This is sheer nonsense. No conductor can divide himself into two people, a time-beater and an interpreter. The interpretation must always be *in* the time-beating itself. There are infinite numbers of ways, for example, of beating two, each way showing a different quality. A conductor should be able to convey all these different qualities with his left arm tied behind his back. He must be able to beat a short, sharp two, which is known as staccato:

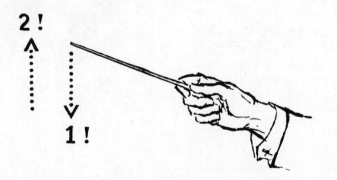

a warm, smooth singing two, which is known as legato:

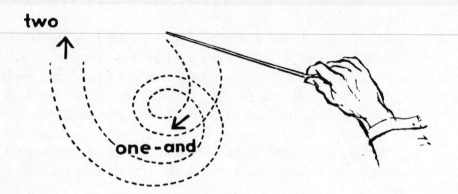

or a broad, sustained two:

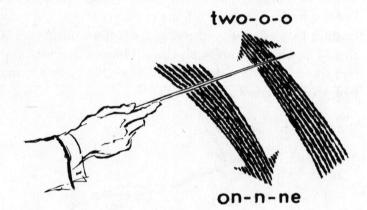

or a light, playful two:

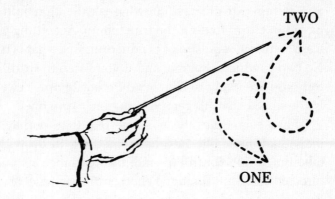

or a dramatic, stormy two:

or any number of other subtle deviations.

However, a conductor cannot beat in a vacuum. He must beat at a certain rate of speed, in what is called a tempo. First he must have the gift of finding the true tempo. According to Wagner, this was the prime requisite of conducting. But what is the *true* tempo? No two conductors agree, and if you listen to six different conductors, you are likely to hear six different tempi. Yet each conductor is convinced that his tempo is the only true one.

It has sometimes been suggested that perhaps a musician's individual metabolic rate has something to do with it, since metabolism would control his rate of breathing, his pulse, and therefore his sense of timing. Whether this is true or not is not yet generally agreed on. So we are left with a situation where conductors become mortal enemies over a tempo, and where music lovers wrangle endlessly about their favorite conductors. Now just to show how differently musicians can conceive the tempo of the same piece, I would like you to listen to a recording of the first few bars of Bach's second *Brandenburg Concerto,* first as conducted by Fritz Reiner:

then as led by Karl Haas:

Slow and measured

and finally as conducted by Pablo Casals:

Very, very fast

Highly controversial; but the main thing is that whatever tempo a conductor takes, he must keep it steady. This is not so easy as it sounds. Most conducting students find it difficult to keep from getting faster or slower.

Of course, very often the conductor wishes *not* to keep a steady beat— to have a free flow instead of a mechanical one. Musicians call this "rubato." The Italian word *rubato* means, literally, "robbed," and the word is used in music in the sense of robbing Peter to pay Paul. In other words, one steals a little time by shortening one beat, and gives it back by lengthening another. In so doing one can create a kind of liberty or free play among the beats which takes it out of the strait jacket of machinelike time-beating. So instead of beating one-two-three-four like a clock:

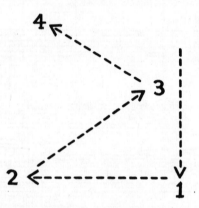

you might shorten one beat and lengthen the other accordingly:

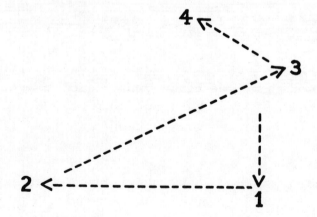

Here, for example, is a bit of Chopin played with no rubato:

L. B. plays piano with no attempt to "interpret":

and now with exaggerated rubato:

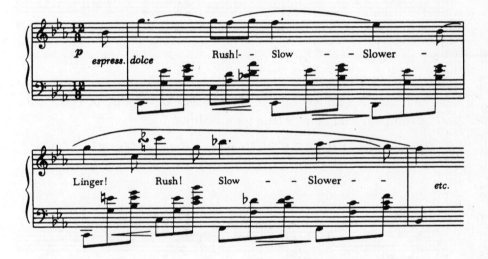

As you can see, rubato can be greatly abused. In fact, unless it is very delicately handled, in a way justified by the style and sense of the music, it can degenerate into the worst kind of sentimentality. With taste, however, it is an indispensable part of the conductor's equipment.

And now, after all that— knowing how to beat, how to show the character of the music in the beat, finding the right tempo, keeping it steady, managing a tasteful rubato— after all that we are still at the beginning of the conductor's job. Now he is faced with the prospect of a sea of knowledge that must be his, and so deeply his that it is automatic. This knowledge begins with being able to read the score.

An orchestral score is a highly complicated thing. A singer has to learn only one line of music, one note at a time:

REQUIEM— Brahms— (III.)— Baritone solo

and maybe (all too rarely!) have some knowledge of the accompaniment. The same is true for a violinist.

VIOLIN CONCERTO— Brahms. Mvt. II

A pianist has to learn many more notes at a time.

PIANO SONATA, OP. 5— Brahms. Mvt. I

But a conductor has to learn and know thoroughly an astonishing number of notes, voices and parts— all at once.

Brahms's FIRST SYMPHONY.

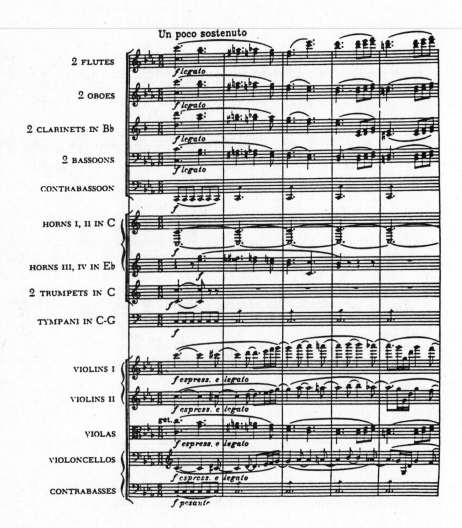

Take this opening bar of Brahms's *First Symphony,* for instance:

There are fifty-five notes in it, being played by one hundred instruments, and the conductor has to know them all or he has no right to ascend the podium in the first place. And this is only one bar out of 1,260 in this symphony.

What does a conductor do when faced with a score like this for the first time? Usually he begins by reading it through more or less superficially, something like racing through a detective story. There is suspense, and the desire to discover how it will all turn out. But what he sees he also hears in his head. People are amazed to discover that a conductor hears a score as he looks at it, but it is true; and the extent to which he can hear the printed notes in his head is in a way a measure of his talent. In this first reading, he must form his own opinion of the cultural and stylistic position of the work. Here a whole other kind of knowledge comes into play: a knowledge of Brahms's period; the atmosphere of his life and of his country; the goals he set himself in his work; the influence of other composers and artists on him— in short, all the cultural background that surrounds his work. In other words, a conductor must be more than a musician; he must be also a kind of artistic historian.

Well, now, he has examined the score swiftly from cover to cover. Now the real work begins. He must take it apart and study all the aspects of it. First of all he sees that the whole orchestra is playing, except for the three trombones, which will enter only in the fourth movement for the big finale. Then he sees that the woodwind instruments— two flutes, two oboes, two clarinets and two bassoons— are all playing the same thing, a descending, double line, making a kind of choir sound.

Now the conductor immediately looks for any other instruments, in any other choir (the brass or strings), that may be playing the same material, or, as musicians say, "doubling" the wind parts. And here he finds it; these two horns are doubling at least part of the line:

and here the violas are doubling all of it:

But he still has not found the melody, the real heart of the matter. This is the other function that our old friend Wagner declared to be especially required of a conductor: the ability to find the melody in this mass of notes. Well, here it is played, as you see, by the first violins, by the second violins an octave lower, and by the cellos an octave lower still.

So we have two elements moving at once, one climbing, the other descending.

This pull of the two lines against each other, tugging in opposite directions, sets up the atmosphere of tension and conflict which will characterize this whole first movement.

But the two lines are not all. There is a long held note in the other two horns growling out the bass.

This note is reinforced by the double basses, which repeat it over and over again, six times per bar.

Then our conductor finds that the kettledrum, or tympany, is doing the same thing as the basses, strengthening them with its penetrating percussion.

And, finally, the trumpets double the bass note up high to help give a brilliant start to the piece.

So the conductor finds three main elements going simultaneously: the two lines tearing at each other over a fateful, ominous series of thuds in the bass. He further finds slur lines over almost all the notes, which tell him that any group of notes lying under one of these curved lines should be played in a connected or *legato* way. All this gives him the clues to the musical meaning of those black dots and lines: dramatic, tense, straining, suffering, doom-ridden.

But now he must decide how fast all this goes. The tempo mark by Brahms is, as you see, *"Un poco sostenuto."* This means "a little sustained" and clearly tells us nothing. Can you measure a rate of speed by these words? No. There is such a thing as a metronome, a mechanical instrument calibrated to various speed-numbers, which clicks off any tempo you want according to the rate of so many beats per minute.

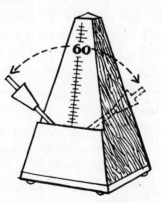

For example, sixty beats per minute means a beat per second, a rather slow tempo. A metronome marking of 152 would indicate a speed of 152 beats per minute, which is bordering on the breakneck.

But Brahms didn't give us a metronome marking, and neither did many other composers. So we are stuck with three Italian words— *un poco sostenuto*— a little bit sustained. Well, at least, we know it must be sustained and therefore not fast. But why, then, didn't he just say slow? What Brahms is getting at is a kind of steady tread, which must be solemn and ominous, and yet not so slow that it will hurt the flow of those two tense lines sounding above it. You see, some of that tension must be achieved through a sense of forward motion. Otherwise the lines won't pull against each other strongly enough.

All this considered, it now devolves upon the conductor to find the true tempo. He may decide to take his cue from the repeated drumbeats, emphasizing the aspect of doom and solemnity. In this case he would favor a more deliberate tempo. Or our conductor might decide on a more forward-going tempo, emphasizing the straining motion of the two melodic lines. Both versions could be called "*un poco sostenuto*"; the difference lies in the conception of the conductor.

Well, now, perhaps our man is ready to conduct page one of the Brahms *First*. No— wait. He still has not considered the letter "f" that appears at the beginning of each part. "F" stands for *forte* and means loud. Even here he is faced with a decision: how loud? If Brahms had wanted it very loud indeed, he would have written two "f's" or three. But no. One "f," just plain loud. There is something of Brahms's classical restraint involved here. It is like *un poco sostenuto*— don't go overboard on the slow tempo or on the volume. So, one forte, loud, but not too loud. And then those little words: *legato*— connected; *espressivo*— expressively; *pesante*— heavy on those bass notes.

Now, is he ready at last to conduct this page? I'm afraid not. Let's take those horn notes, for instance, playing the descending line. They happen to lie in the high, brilliant register of the horn, and have a way of pealing out like church bells— which is all right, if it doesn't drown out the other instruments. And here comes the whole problem of balancing the orchestra. He must realize that in order to have real balance, the horns are going to have to start playing in a slightly reduced version of that one "f"—

forte— in order not to come clanging in, upsetting those smooth, connected lines we're talking about. Then, as the horn line descends, it moves into an area of the horn range which is less proclamatory, and so the horns can then increase their volume to match the rest of the orchestra. This is only one of the many such subleties that is the conductor's responsibility, since Brahms indicated nothing in the score about the horns varying in volume.

Naturally, the ability to balance an orchestra properly depends also on the conductor's knowledge of the orchestral instruments themselves: their capacities, their exact ranges, their weaknesses, and their particular colors. He must know exactly what shades of sound he wants, and then know how to ask the players to produce them. For example, the trumpets belong to a family of brass which is naturally strident and piercing. But at the climax of the last movement of Brahms's *First,* when the brass sings out the great chorale theme, the color must not be strident and piercing, even though it is very loud. It must be a singing sound, like a great organ. It is the conductor's job to see that the brass sings. Similarly, he must know how to make the strings play percussively, which is contrary to *their* nature. He must know how to evoke different singing sounds from the violins, by using a fast vibrato, or a slow vibrato, or using very little bow, or using a lot of bow. He must decide whether he wants a pizzicato produced by plucking the string with the hard tip of the finger, which will give one color, or with the soft, fleshy part of the finger, which gives a whole different color. He must know how to ask for "thicker" or "thinner" sounds from the oboes and clarinets, for various differences in percussion sounds; the list is endless.

This formidable knowledge of his must even include a capacity for anticipating the mistakes any orchestra may make, which he can do if he knows the natural bad habits that players commonly fall into. For example, players of music have an unconscious habit of making a crescendo (that is, getting louder) when the music goes up, and doing the opposite— a diminuendo— on a descending line. What will happen to Brahms if they do this? Remember those two contrary melodic lines on page one? If the descending line weakens, the whole pull and strain of the two lines disappear.

These are only some of thousands of such subtle details. The study of a great score is endless, and a conductor is eternally a student. Toscanini in his eighties studied just as hard before he conducted the *Eroica* for the five hundredth time as he did when he began his career. And he got just as nervous before he took the stage as he always had.

So in a way, our conductor will never be completely ready to conduct page one of Brahms's *First*; but let's assume that he is reasonably ready now. He still has 165 pages more to go, and they are pages of even greater complexity and decision-making. And when he has gone through all of these matters of balance, dynamics, tempo, expression, style, concept, and cultural background, then he is ready to conduct a good, routine performance of Brahms's *First*. He will play the symphony as Brahms wrote it, with satisfying tempi; no melody will be drowned out by its accompaniment; the orchestra will play in tune (if he has a good ear); and it will be a faithful rendition, if possibly unexciting.

For the qualities that distinguish *great* conductors lie far beyond and above what we have spoken of. We now begin to deal with the intangibles, the deep magical aspect of conducting. It is the mystery of relationships— conductor and orchestra bound together by the tiny but powerful split second. How can I describe to you the magic of the moment of beginning a piece of music? There is only one possible fraction of a second that feels exactly right for starting. There is a wait while the orchestra readies itself and collects its powers; while the conductor concentrates his whole will and force toward the work in hand; while the audience quiets down, and the last cough has died away. There is no slight rustle of a program book; the instruments are poised and— bang! That's it. One second later, it is too late, and the magic has vanished.

This psychological timing is constantly in play throughout the performance of music. It means that a great conductor is one who has great sensitivity to the flow of time; who makes one note move to the next in exactly the right way and at the right instant. For music, as we said, exists in the medium of time. It is time itself that must be carved up, molded and remolded until it becomes, like a statue, an existing shape and form. This is the hardest to do. For a symphony is not like a statue, which can be viewed all at once, or bit by bit at leisure, in one's own chosen time. With music, we are trapped in time. Each note is gone as soon as it has sounded, and it never can be recontemplated or heard again at the particular instant of rightness. It is always too late for a second look.

So the conductor is a kind of sculptor whose element is time instead of marble; and in sculpting it, he must have a superior sense of proportion and relationship. He must judge the largest rhythms, the whole phraseology of a work. He must conquer the form of a piece not only in the sense of form as a mold, but form in its deepest sense, knowing and controlling where the music relaxes, where it begins to accumulate tension, where the greatest tension is reached, where it must ease up to gather strength for the next lap, where it unloads that strength.

These are the intangibles of conducting, the mysteries that no conductor can learn or acquire. If he has a natural faculty for deep perception, it will increase and deepen as he matures. If he hasn't, he will always remain a pretty good conductor. But even the pretty good conductor must have one more attribute in his personality, without which all the mechanics and knowledge and perception are useless; and that is the power to *communicate* all this to his orchestra— through his arms, face, eyes, fingers, and whatever vibrations may flow from him. If he uses a baton, the baton itself must be a living thing, charged with a kind of electricity, which makes it an instrument of meaning in its tiniest movement. If he does not use a baton, his hands must do the job with equal clarity. But baton or no baton, his gestures must be first and always meaningful in terms of the music.

So we see that communication with the orchestra requires a technique which is physical. You know how certain emotions produce physical reflexes in us. If we are pleased, certain muscles around the mouth move involuntarily and we smile. It is the same in conducting. The feelings evoked by the music cause certain muscular reactions, and these, given back to the orchestra through conducting, can re-evoke those feelings in the players.

(Of course there must also be a certain amount of talk at a rehearsal; there are things that cannot be explained by gesture alone.

But long, romantic speeches about the beauty-meanings of a piece, with digressions about forests and babbling brooks, are usually of no earthly use.)

The chief element in the conductor's technique of communication is the preparation. Everything must be shown to the orchestra *before* it happens. Once the player is playing the note, it is too late. So the conductor always has to be at least a beat or two ahead of the orchestra. And he must hear two things at the same time: what the players are doing at any moment, and what they are about to do a moment later. Therefore, the basic trick is in the preparatory upbeat. If our conductor is back again on page one of Brahms's *First*, he must show, in his silent upbeat, the character of the music which is about to sound. Whether he thinks of it as tense and agitated, or weighty and doom-ridden, his upbeat should show this, in order to enable the orchestra players to respond in kind. It is exactly like breathing: the preparation is like an inhalation, and the music sounds as an exhalation. We all have to inhale in order to speak, for example; all verbal expression is exhaled. So it is with music: we inhale on the upbeat and sing out a phrase of music, then inhale again and breathe out the next phrase. A conductor who breathes with the music has gone far in acquiring a technique.

But the conductor must not only make his orchestra play; he must make them want to play. He must exalt them, lift them, start their adrenalin pouring, either through cajoling or demanding or raging. But however he does it, he must make the orchestra love the music as he loves it. It is not so much imposing his will on them like a dictator; it is more like projecting his feelings around him so that they reach the last man in the second violin section. And when this happens— when one hundred men share his feelings, exactly, simultaneously, responding as one to each rise and fall of the music, to each point of arrival and departure, to each little inner pulse— then there is a human identity of feeling that has no equal elsewhere. It is the closest thing I know to love itself. On this current of love the conductor can communicate at the deepest levels with his players, and ultimately with his audience. He may shout and rant and curse and insult his players at rehearsal—

as some of our greatest conductors are famous for doing— but if there is this love, the conductor and his orchestra will remain knit together through it all and function as one.

Well, there is our ideal conductor. And perhaps the chief requirement of all is that he be humble before the composer; that he never interpose himself between the music and the audience; that all his efforts, however strenuous or glamorous, be made in the service of the composer's meaning— the music itself, which, after all, is the whole reason for the conductor's existence.

(The telecast concluded with a short, unprepared rehearsal of the fourth movement of Brahms's First Symphony.)

AMERICAN
MUSICAL COMEDY

TELECAST: OCTOBER 7, 1956

Leonard Bernstein:

The glittering world of musical theater is an enormous field that includes everything from your nephew's high-school pageant to *Götterdämmerung*. And somehow in that great mass of song and dance and drama lies something called the American musical comedy— a magic phrase. We seem to be addicted to it; we pay enormous sums to attend it; we discuss it at breakfast and at cocktail parties with a passion otherwise reserved for elections and the Dodgers. We anticipate a new musical comedy of Rodgers and Hammerstein or of Frank Loesser with the same excitement and partisan feeling as Milan used to await a new Puccini opera, or Vienna the latest Brahms symphony. We hear on all sides that America has given the world a new form— unique, vital, inimitable. Yet no one seems to be able to tell us what this phenomenon is. Why is *Guys and Dolls* unique? What makes *South Pacific* different? Why can't Europe imitate *Pajama Game*? Is *My Fair Lady* a milestone along the road to a new art form?

We are going to try to answer these questions for you, and try to find out how the two thousand or so musicals that have opened on Broadway in the last century have developed into this special, exciting thing we know today as American musical comedy.

Well, first, let's define the area which we are investigating. In that vast field of musical theater, we can discern a continuum— a kind of ruler— by which we can mark out the difference between one show and another. Let us think of this continuum as operating between two poles: the variety show at one end and the opera at the other. Between these two we can account for every other form:

Variety Show	(Music Hall, Vaudeville, etc.)
Revue	(e.g. *Ziegfeld Follies*)
Operetta	(e.g. *Naughty Marietta*)
Comic Opera	(e.g. *H.M.S. Pinafore*)
Opera Buffa	(e.g. *Barber of Seville*)
Opéra Comique	(e.g. *Carmen*)
Grand Opera	(e.g. *Pagliacci*)
Wagnerian Music Drama	(e.g. *Die Walküre*)

— and all the rest. All of these occupy a middle ground between the two poles of variety show and opera and, to some degree or other, may resemble either or both extremes.

Now, what is it that separates these two extremes so widely? Well, there are *two* main differences. First, of course, is the difference in intention. A variety show aims to please, and nothing more; an opera, on the other hand, has an artistic intention, which is to enrich and ennoble the audience by inducing lofty emotions in them. Then there is a difference of kind: a variety show is a packaged collection of songs and dances, skits and sketches, acrobatic turns, dog acts, and what not, put together with no unifying thread other than variety itself; whereas an opera has a story to tell— a plot— and aims to further this plot *through* the use of music.

All these other forms we have seen vacillate between variety and opera. The more a show gets away from pure diversion, the more it tries to engage the interest and emotion of the audience, the closer it slides toward opera. And the more a show uses music to further its plot, the closer it moves toward the same pole.

Now just how does a plot get furthered by the use of music? There are a number of ways— ballet, underscoring, choral devices, etc.— but the most common technique for telling your story musically is the recitative, or *recitativo*, a word which you certainly know as somehow associated with opera, but perhaps are a bit foggy about. What is this recitative, anyway? Let's suppose I am in a musical show whose plot calls on me to inform my wife that chicken has gone up three cents a pound. In an ordinary musical show I would simply say to her, "Chicken is up three cents a pound," and my wife would burst forth then, singing a lament about the high cost of living. But in an opera, I would sing my line, and I would have to resort to the recitative— let's say, in the style of Mozart:

L. B. sings:

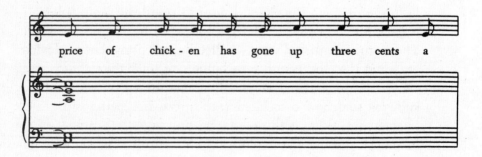

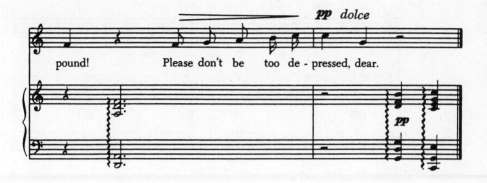

This recitative has no real musical value and is very close to plain talk except for an intermittent piano chord. Nor is it particularly descriptive of my feelings about chicken. Of course I could get more dramatic in the style of Verdi:

— or Wagner:

But no matter how expressive I get, I am still singing something of less musical importance than the song itself which my wife will sing immediately afterward. It's the song, or the number, that will get the applause, no matter how heart-breakingly I tell of the price of chicken. The function of my recitative is to set up the situation for the song.

By this time you're probably wondering what all this has to do with musical comedy. After all, these recitatives I've been discussing all seem so fancy and operatic, the very opposite of what we think of as the Broadway spirit. But there's a strong relation here because musical comedy belongs somewhere in that middle ground we spoke of between variety show and opera. And over the last hundred years there has been a continuous trend, slow but sure, from one pole toward the other, from simple diversion toward art, through our way of using recitatives and ballet and underscoring and the rest. Now let's see if we can follow that trend.

It all began in 1866, ninety years ago, with a great extravaganza called *The Black Crook*, a smash hit containing a show-stopper called "You Naughty, Naughty Men." It was a comedy song having nothing to do with the plot, but which served only to amuse the audience while the scenery was being changed.

Production number:

"YOU NAUGHTY, NAUGHTY MEN"
Music— G. Bicknell   Words— T. Kennick

Moderato

I will ne - ver more de - ceive you, or of hap - pi - ness be - reave you, But I'll

die a maid to grieve you, oh! you naught-y, naught- y men   You may

talk of love and sigh - ing, say for us you're near - ly dy - ing, All the

Nothing very terrific, is it? But it's important, because *The Black Crook* is historically considered to be the first American musical comedy.

Actually, it was a musical comedy by sheer accident and is in no way related to what we now think of as musical comedy, except that it was the first variety show to acquire a plot. When I say "by accident" I mean it literally. It was a freak. Someone named Barras had written a Germanic melodrama called *The Black Crook*, which called for no music at all. It was his first play, and luckily his last. A producer named Wheatley was mad enough to buy it for presentation at Niblo's Garden, New York City. Meanwhile, a French ballet company had arrived on these shores to find the theater where they were to dance burned to the ground. Then the great idea was born: in order to provide a theater for the ballet company, it was decided to merge the two productions and add the wonders of music and dance to *The Black Crook*. And so Niblo's Garden was transformed into a mighty music hall. *The Black Crook* was attached to song and dance with spit and chewing gum, and the show was on.

It lasted five and a half hours, and nobody left. They loved it. There were Gothic melodrama and dancing girls in tights, and comedy songs, and long speeches by Stalacta, Queen of the Golden Realm. There were gnomes and demons and Zamiel the arch-fiend, and Swiss peasant maids— all mishmashed together. And it turned out to be one of the great hits of all time, running a year and a half in New York and for twenty-five years more on the road.

How could this have happened? Well, it was a lot for your money: drama plus songs plus dance plus spectacle *plus* legs (there was such a controversy about *them* that anybody who was anybody had to be able to say that he had seen that wicked show). What can *we* say of *The Black Crook?* Not much. Its score is a mélange of uninspired songs like the one we just heard, and dance music of similar value— like this one, called "March of the Amazons."

L. B. plays piano:

Arr. by Emil Stiyler by permission of David Costa,
Maître de Danse.

Or this dull little number, called "The Black Crook Waltz":

— which was, however, bolstered up by a grand introduction:

which makes the tune sound even sillier, once it finally arrives. There was also the usual piano-tremolo type of incidental music that we still recall from silent-movie days:

All these pieces just followed one another, loosely strung together like the German plot and the French ballet and the American comedy songs. In other words, it was a high-class, expensive variety show, plot or no plot.

Of course, many people in 1866 thought they were getting *Art*: after all, ballet is art, and fancy stage spectacles can sometimes be art. But it was so considered mainly because it was imported. In those days, anything good in the art world had to be foreign. Real art, in the sense of a creative form growing out of healthy native roots, did not come into the question.

The first step in the direction of native roots was taken around 1890, with the appearance of a show called *A Trip to Chinatown*, another great hit of the nineteenth century. It was this show which proved that a musical could have an American story, out of which could come the American songs— like this one, which I'm sure you'll all recognize, even though it's almost 73 years old.

Male quartet:

"THE BOWERY"— Music: Percy Grant, Words: Chas. H. Hoyt

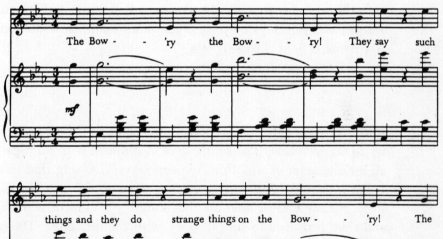

It's a nice song, but the trouble is that it's just stuck into the plot arbitrarily, with no regard for what is known as integration.

Now, this whole business of integration is a tough one. It demands that a song come out of the situation in the story and make sense with the given characters. In a way, the whole growth of our musical comedy can be seen through the growth of integration. We *have* made astonishing progress, though even today we are all familiar with the kind of show in which songs are forced into the script with a shoe horn— where Boy meets Girl, for instance, and Boy says nothing much more than "How do you do? My name is Sam.   "

And that passes for integration. But *A Trip to Chinatown* didn't try to do even that. The songs were introduced with no regard at all for character or situation. Someone says, "Do sing that quartet I like so much." And the quartet gets sung. Or in a restaurant scene someone says, "I know that song the orchestra is playing," and then proceeds to sing it along with the orchestra. The good thing is that some of these songs turned out to be quite fine— like "The Bowery," and another one, still fondly remembered:

L. B. sings:

"REUBEN AND CYNTHIA"—
Arr: Percy Grant, Words: Chas. H. Hoyt

This was already a folk song at the time it was used in *A Trip to Chinatown;* but that doesn't diminish the fact that an *American* song was being used in an American story. And not only did it have an American *story,* but it had American speech patterns as well. In other words, the characters talked like people everybody knew, *in the vernacular.*

Well, now that we had discovered America, and also discovered the fact that a musical show could have a plot, or a book, things began to pop. Only now that book was going to have to be something a little better than *A Trip to Chinatown;* and, what is more, the lyrics, or the *sung* words, were going to have to be more literate. For years now Americans had been exposed to the comic operas of those great geniuses, Gilbert and Sullivan, and automatically a standard had been set for excellence of lyrics and music. Their influence changed our tastes in such a way that Trips to Chinatown would never again be possible.

For Gilbert and Sullivan, along with those other geniuses, Johann Strauss and Offenbach, had led the American public straight into the arms of operetta. All three were national versions of the same thing: Gilbert and Sullivan with their British comic opera, Offenbach with his French *opéra bouffe,* and Strauss with his Viennese operetta. They all boasted interesting books, stylish music and literate lyrics. And so at the turn of the century we entered a great operetta period, which bloomed up through the First World War and has been with us ever since.

Such operettas as *The Merry Widow* by Lehar swept the Broadway public off its feet and started a long line of them by middle-European composers like Rudolph Friml, Sigmund Romberg, Emmerich Kalman, and the rest. But the great American hero of the operetta was Victor Herbert:

(At this point a soprano soloist and chorus sing "The Italian Street Song" from Herbert's Naughty Marietta.)

Anyone would know immediately that this is operetta and not musical comedy. *Naughty Marietta* is unmistakable. So is *Eileen* unmistakably operetta, and so is *The Red Mill,* and all the others.

Why do we know these are operettas and not musical comedies?

Because one and all they are exotic in flavor. *Naughty Marietta* is
bathed in Creole atmosphere, with Italian fixings; *Eileen* is pure
Irish, and *The Red Mill* is Dutch. This is no accident; it is one
of the prerequisites of operetta that it be fancy and somewhat
remote from the audience's experience. The characters must be
unfamiliar and sometimes improbable. The language they use is
stilted and overelegant. They do not speak the vernacular, in spite
of the fact that these works were being written in America for
Americans. This is true of all the operettas that followed: *The
Desert Song, The Firefly, New Moon*— it's a long list.

But dated and clumsy as they seem now, they performed a great
service in the early years of this century. They accustomed the
audiences to good songs and good lyrics, to stories that were fresh
and charming, but most of all to a new level of musical accom-
plishment. For the operetta score was no mere collection of songs.
It was musically elaborate, closer to opera, even containing finales,
with everybody *singing* his way through the plot, vocalizing different sentiments at the same time— the real contrapuntal McCoy.
Thus operetta became part of the audience's growing up and coming to understand and enjoy a certain amount of musical complexity. As a result, Broadway audiences, which had not been trained to
enjoy grand opera, were being prepared, through operetta, for
the more ambitious musical comedies we have today.

Meantime, just across the street, so to speak, the vernacular was
blooming away on its own in the plotless musical theater. This
was the heyday of the variety show; burlesque was flourishing,
with Weber and Fields; and the names in lights were Lillian Rus-
sell, Anna Held, Marie Dressler, and the glorified Ziegfeld girls;
and a new idea was taking the town by storm— the revue. Actually, a revue is a variety show, in that it is a collection of songs and
acts without a story. But the revue introduced a unifying thread,
however flimsy, that could hold all these acts together— some
thread like Paris, or Zanzibar, or Greenwich Village.

Secondly, it introduced the element of topical satire, sketches
that spoofed the fashionable life of the city. Take-offs of successful plays and operas, sly references to current scandals, parodies
of new fads, local jokes— all these are still today the mainstay of

our revues. Whereas then they spoofed Gounod's *Faust* and Sarah Bernhardt, today we spoof Menotti's operas and Marlon Brando. But certainly the main contribution of the revue was the introduction to the theater of *musical* vernacular— by which I mean jazz. And the first great contributor was an unforgettable revue called *Watch Your Step*, which opened at the New Amsterdam Theater in 1914. The hero of all this was Irving Berlin, who provided such delicious ragtime songs that the American musical theater and jazz were thenceforth wedded forever.

(Singers and orchestra perform three numbers: "Simple Melody," "The Syncopated Walk," and "Show Us How to Do the Fox-trot" from Berlin's revue Watch Your Step.*)*

But what has all this to do with musical comedy? After all, a revue has no plot, no *book,* and the book is the essential basis of musical comedy. Ah, but there is a very important relation. Musical comedy has learned a lot from revues. It has learned to treat its book in the manner of a variety show; it has learned to take variety and unify it. This is one of the great secrets of our magic formula: to give an audience a continuous and convincing story, yet to have them leave the theater feeling that they have also had a rounded evening of fun— dancing, comedy scenes, emotional singing, gay singing, pretty girls— the works, but somehow all cleverly integrated into a good story. Variety in unity: that was the key lesson that musical comedy learned from the revue, a big step forward.

And so the childhood of the American musical theater came to an end, and we embarked, full of confidence and resources, on our adolescence. That adolescence was typically awkward, overenergetic, and more than a little wild; but it was not so painful as most, largely owing to the wealth of talent that now began to appear. Irving Berlin was already an old master; now came Jerome Kern, a rare melodist; and the decade of the Twenties was to see the rise of Vincent Youmans, Cole Porter, Richard Rodgers, and George Gershwin. With this sensational array of talent, the musical theater grew like any growing boy, building on its now solid accomplishments: the acceptance of plot into musical entertainment, the acceptance of American themes, of talk and music in the vernacular, the highly elevated standards in the music and lyrics, and the sense of variety within unity.

Now it was about time that musical comedies began paying a little much needed attention to the subject of integrating songs into the plot. Times had changed since *The Black Crook*. Take a great hit show from the Twenties like *Oh, Kay!*, for instance. This was the first noteworthy product of George Gershwin and his brother Ira; it had a book by *real* writers— P. G. Wodehouse and Guy Bolton— and it starred none other than Gertrude Lawrence. *Oh, Kay!*, which was about bootleggers on Long Island, is considered a typical Twenties musical comedy on the most sophisticated level. And yet, when we see how the songs were integrated, or rather not integrated, in it, it seems a bit naïve.

For example, Gershwin had written a lovely song called "Someone to Watch Over Me." I'm sure you all know it. Now, I have a sneaky feeling that this song was written *before* the book was written, instead of having evolved logically out of the book, because it doesn't *quite* fit the situation in which it was sung. It almost fits, but not quite. The situation is this: girl has met boy and has fallen in love with him. But he is committed to marry another. Girl sits on settee and gives the cue line: "Oh, I know that I shall meet him again some day." She then plunges into the verse, or introductory section, of the song, in which she sings about "A certain lad I've had in mind." *"Had in mind"*! She's just played three scenes with him! Anyway, she goes on: "Looking everywhere, haven't found him yet." *"Haven't found him yet"*! Then what has the whole first act been about? But, as they said in the mad, gay Twenties, what's the diff? The lyrics are so distinguished and fresh, and the tune is a knockout.

(Singer and orchestra perform "Someone to Watch Over Me.")

American theater music was certainly acquiring its own character. This could never have existed in an operetta. It's much too easy, intimate, conversational, *friendly,* for an operetta. In other words, it's a great American popular song. But it's not exactly what you'd call part of the plot line of *Oh, Kay!*

My favorite example of nonintegration in *Oh, Kay!* concerns a

wonderful little ditty called "Clap Yo' Hands," which is wedged
into the score by a device no more subtle than those used in *A
Trip to Chinatown*. Only there's a twist. The authors *know* they
are wedging, that the song has no real function except to provide
fun, and so they resort to making fun of *themselves* and point up
the fact with high-handed wit.

What happens is this: the chief comic, Potter by name, is trying
to spread cheer during a gloomy situation. He turns to the inevitable line of chorus girls and says, "It's the philosophy of sun-
shine, girls. I learned it at the knee of my old mammy. Do you
want to hear a Mammy song?" But here's the twist: "No!" scream
the girls in chorus. "Very well, then," says Potter, "I'll sing you the
song she used to sing to me."

(L. B. sings a few bars of "Clap Yo' Hands")

It's wonderful fun, an exciting tune, a real Gershwin invention.
And it has nothing to do with the plot, nothing at all. But the fact
that a joke is made out of its having nothing to do with the plot
reveals a new level of sophistication which had been reached in
the Twenties. At least they *knew* that what they were doing was
pure revue technique and could laugh at themselves for it. And
that was a step forward in itself.

Then came the crash of '29 and the depression. There were
suddenly fewer productions and fewer ticket buyers to attend
them. On top of that, the movies developed sound, and the people
began running to movies instead, where escape was cheaper. The
mass audience had shrunk, and the theater was again forced upward in its scale of values, in order to please a smaller but more
discriminating public.

So, if the Twenties could be called the adolescence of our musical comedy, then the Thirties certainly represented its sober
young manhood. The tenor of the times dictated seriousness.
America had become suddenly adult, consciously involved with
government and social problems. This certainly doesn't mean that
our musicals stopped being funny and entertaining; it's only that
they veered more in the direction of social satire. In fact, the most

serious social satire of the period was the hilariously funny *Of Thee I Sing*. The appearance of this great Gershwin show in 1931 signalized the tone of the Thirties. It had a solid, tremendously witty book by George Kaufman and Morrie Ryskind, a book, by the way, which was the first musical play to win the Pulitzer Prize. Imagine the Pulitzer Prize going to a musical-comedy book! It's unthinkable in terms of any show before *Of Thee I Sing*, but we were growing up.

All the points we have noticed in the long maturing of the musical comedy now bear fruit in *Of Thee I Sing*. A marvelous story, serious and funny in a way no show had ever been before: glorious songs, perfectly integrated into the scheme; a highly American subject; natural American speech; sharp, brilliant lyrics; an all-over unity of style embodying wide variety— in other words, this show marks a point of culmination in our history.

What fascinates me about *Of Thee I Sing* is the brilliant way in which it uses operetta technique, of all things, to produce this highly original American show. And as we said, an operetta score demands a trained and thorough musician, not just a songwriter. Gershwin more than qualified. There is a first-act finale with lyrics in the great tradition of Gilbert and Sullivan, and so elaborate that it can be compared, blow by blow, with the first-act finale of *The Mikado*, one of Gilbert's finest.

The situations are almost parallel in the two works: Boy has met Girl and won her; and the action centers on the interruption of the love festivities by the Other Woman, in one case ugly Katisha, in the other, beauteous Diana Devereaux.

(The first-act finales of Of Thee I Sing *and of* The Mikado *are presented, switching back and forth between them, section by section, to show the similarity of situation, the matched excellence of the lyrics, the equality of wit and technique.)*

But why, then, is *Of Thee I Sing* a musical comedy and not an operetta? After all, it's musically elaborate: it has counterpoint, it uses underscoring, and it has reams of recitative. Well, it *is* a musical comedy because it meets all the requirements that have been set up by musical comedy's development: it has a super-

American theme, the characters are not remote or exotic— although the situation is pretty wild— and it is, both verbally and musically, in the vernacular. Of course it has borrowed freely from operetta, in *technique;* but its soul is the soul of musical comedy.

So the question of musical comedy versus operetta is a more complex one than you perhaps imagined. For example, *Show Boat* is an operetta. Here you have a beloved work by Kern and Hammerstein which has as American a theme as we've ever had, but deals with an aspect of America which is far from the experience of the very Broadway public for whom it was created. Remember that New York is the garden in which this whole history grew, so what we mean by an American theme is one which does not seem foreign to that New York public. *Show Boat*, being about flavorsome life on the old Mississippi, is in that sense a true operetta.

Besides, it employs highly regional language, not what we mean by "the vernacular." Don't mistake me: by vernacular I don't mean only tough Broadway lingo; I mean a familiar, easy American speech pattern, not thick Southern dialect. So by this standard as well, *Show Boat* is basically an operetta. So is *The King and I*, which is usually called a musical comedy, and so are *Fanny* and *Carousel* too— all operettas. They are written, it is true, in the most up-to-date Broadway manner, utilizing all the advances in taste and technique, but operettas none the less.

Musically, too, they are operettas in that they don't employ the *musical* vernacular of Broadway. In other words, they don't use jazz— urban jazz, which is the essence of American popular music. The songs of these shows are closer to art songs than they are to Tin Pan Alley.

On the other hand, a show like Cole Porter's *DuBarry Was a Lady* has a story about Louis Quinze and Mme. DuBarry and the court of Versailles— all very fancy and foreign. Yet it is no operetta, because it is so full of jazz, and delivered in the toughest vernacular by Ethel Merman and Bert Lahr. It is eighteenth-century France on Forty-fourth Street; and the whole fun of it is implicit in Bert Lahr's playing the role of Louis the Fifteenth. Besides, no show can be an operetta if Merman is in it; she is Broadway in person, whether she's in a powdered wig or a wigwam.

("Ooh-La-La" from Dubarry Was a Lady *is contrasted with Herbert's "Thine Alone" from* Eileen.)

Through this merging of operetta with revue techniques something new had happened: music had gotten onto a more serious plane. As long as there were only songs in a musical comedy it had been enough to be just a songwriter. But now the songwriter found himself called upon to be a serious composer, able to write extended musical sequences, counterpoint, orchestration— in other words, much more than just a thirty-two-bar tune. Light and serious music were coming closer together.

One serious composer, Marc Blitzstein, had even invaded Broadway with his odd, original opera, *The Cradle Will Rock.* Then Kurt Weill had brought his whole German training to Broadway in such works as *Lady in the Dark.* George Gershwin himself, who had been diligently studying counterpoint and fugue, had invaded the opera house with *Porgy and Bess,* a grand opera, written to be sung from start to finish, which means that Gershwin had entered the arena of serious composition.

But most of our show composers were still only thirty-two-bar songwriters, as most of them are to this day. It was not their fault that the musical comedy had grown so fast. And so, realizing that they couldn't do this big job alone, they began to call in that small army of helpers who are today a trademark in every show production: the orchestrators and arrangers who are responsible for writing all the in-betweenies, the connective tissue, the ballets, musical links for scene changes, overtures, interludes— in other words, everything but the tunes themselves.

Of course it is always, and always will be, the tunes themselves that make or break a show score— and yet I feel much too little credit is given to that small army, especially to those subcomposers who turn a series of songs into a unified score, who make it all sound like a "work." For years you would find their names in small print in the program book, buried among the wig credits and Creco soap. Nowadays they get more attention, but people are still not aware of the phenomenal job they do.

Now that we had this small army, it was possible to do all kinds of new and elaborate things in our shows— chiefly ballet. Ever since 1936, when Rodgers and Hart came up with *On Your Toes,* dancing has come into its own as a plot-furthering medium. In this show, Rodgers and Hart devised a scenario for a ballet called "Slaughter on Tenth Avenue" which has not only its own ballet plot, but also participates climactically in the plot of the whole show. This scenario calls for Ray Bolger to keep dancing for his very life, even after the ballet story is over, since two gangsters are waiting in box seats to let him have it the moment he stops.

(A passage from "Slaughter on Tenth Avenue" is danced.)

This ballet, choreographed by George Balanchine, broke ground for the building of a whole tradition of plot-dancing, for all the action ballets, love ballets, decision ballets, dream ballets and passage-of-time ballets that we have almost come to expect now, after such shows as *Oklahoma!, On the Town* and *Guys and Dolls.* In other words, choreographers like Agnes De Mille, Jerome Robbins and Michael Kidd have become almost as important to our form as the authors and composers and directors; and the whole look and sound of musical comedy has been radically changed.

Which brings us neatly up to modern times.

For the last fifteen years we have been enjoying the greatest period our musical theater has ever known. In these last fifteen years we have finished with young manhood and entered the prime of life. Some of our shows of this period are already young classics: *Pal Joey, Annie Get Your Gun, Oklahoma!, South Pacific, Guys and Dolls, Kiss Me, Kate.* Some people say that the reason for this spurt has been our great prosperity; others say that it is due to American know-how, that world-famous quality of ours.

I don't much like either of these theories, because they don't regard the essential root of it all— the creative spirit. And that is the main reason for our success with musical comedies: they are extravagantly creative. Each one is a surprise; nobody ever knows what new twists and treatments and styles will appear next. There seems to be no limit to our creative energy, or to our reservoir of creators. Gershwin and Hart and Kern and Youmans have died but have not remained unsupplanted. Rodgers found a great new partner in Hammerstein; Ira Gershwin found the tremendously gifted Harold Arlen.

Then along came a new great: Frank Loesser. Five minutes later, it seemed, there were two young Loessers named Ross and Adler, who were turning out material in his style. A marvelous show called *Finian's Rainbow* introduced Burton Lane as a remarkable new composer. Arthur Schwartz, Harold Rome and Jule Styne have made charming contributions. The team of Lerner and Loewe, which gave us *Brigadoon,* hit the jackpot with *My Fair Lady.* And Berlin, Porter, and Rodgers are still very much with us. We're swimming in talent.

Talent has changed everything. For instance, talent has enabled Rodgers and Hammerstein to take the best elements of opera, operetta, revue, vaudeville, and all the rest, and blend them into something quite original. Perhaps the best example of this is *South Pacific,* which many people regard as our supreme achievement in musical comedy. It is as though a new strain has been cross-bred out of the past.

When the Seabees are singing "There is Nothing Like a Dame," or when Nellie sings "I'm Gonna Wash That Man Right Out of My Hair," then it is a musical comedy in our best tradition; but when Bloody Mary sings "Bali Ha'i," it is a romantic operetta, in our best tradition. And somehow it all works like a charm, smooth and utterly professional. No more stylistic hash. No more stringing numbers together. No more sticking in of prefabricated songs, whether they suit the action or not.

Just compare the integration of songs as we saw it in *Oh, Kay!* with the way "Some Enchanted Evening" is introduced in *South Pacific.* The song occurs in the first scene, where Nellie and Emile are falling in love and are uncertain as to whether they ought to. In the process of getting to know each other better, she has just sung him a song revealing her nature— "A Cockeyed Optimist"— and when it is over, she speaks:

Singer-actors:

> NELLIE:
> *Want to know anything else about me?*
> EMILE:
> *Yes, you say you are a fugitive. When you joined the Navy, what were you running away from?*

L. B.:

Here the orchestra sneaks in, giving us a hint of her feelings.

Singer-actors:

> NELLIE:
> *Gosh, I don't know. It was more like running to something. I wanted to see what the world was like— outside Little Rock, I mean. And I wanted to meet different kinds of people and find out if I like them better. And I'm finding out.*
> EMILE:
> *Would you like some cognac?*
> NELLIE:
> *I'd love some.*

L. B.:

It is in the poised moment of this brandy-pouring that the miracle happens. Rodgers and Hammerstein take advantage of the lovers' temporary separation to fashion a double soliloquy, in which each of the pair can *sing* his or her thoughts; yet it is neither a song, as such, nor a recitative. And still it performs the functions of both.

Nellie and Emile sing the double soliloquy:

> NELLIE:
> *Wonder how I'd feel, living on a hillside, looking on an ocean, beautiful and still.*

EMILE:
This is what I need, this is what I've longed for, someone young and smiling climbing up my hill!
NELLIE:
We are not alike; probably I'd bore him. He's a cultured Frenchman— I'm a little hick.
EMILE:
Younger men than I, officers and doctors, probably pursue her— she could have her pick.
NELLIE:
Wonder why I feel jittery and jumpy! I am like a schoolgirl waiting for a dance.
EMILE:
Can I ask her now? I am like a schoolboy! What will be her answer? Do I have a chance?

L.B., as orchestra continues:

We are now standing firmly on operatic ground, since the plot is being furthered by singing, and doing it better than dialogue could in this case. But what is happening now? The lovers are standing, brandy in hand, tense, in love, fighting it. And this is told us, neither by dialogue *nor* by singing, but more eloquently still by the orchestra alone.

(Orchestra plays alone up to climax.)

L. B., after orchestra diminishes:

Thus we are made ready for the introduction of the "big song." A few more lines, over music, lead directly to the fulfillment of "Some Enchanted Evening."

(Emile sings "Some Enchanted Evening")

You see how carefully woven all this is. There is nothing so bald as a cue line and then bang— into the song. They have snuck up on it, with elaborate musical preparation. We have been weaving in and out of music, sometimes sung, sometimes underscored, sometimes with orchestra only, so that when the big song finally does appear, there is no sudden jolt from speech to song, as there always used to be. And this was accomplished by none other than our old friend recitative, a new kind of recitative, based on simple American song forms, and resulting in a lovely double soliloquy. Our colloquial American speech does not like recitation; it is far too rhythmic and accentuated a language to be so free-floating. But Rodgers and Hammerstein, by using this new song style of recitative, are now able to further plot by singing without seeming ridiculously operatic. Again, our musical comedy has moved toward opera but *in our own way.*

What does all this add up to? Simply this: that the American musical theater has come a long way, borrowing this from opera, that from revue, the other from operetta, something else from vaudeville— and mixing all the elements into something quite new, but something which has been steadily moving in the direction of opera.

Certain elements may get more emphasis in one show, and other elements in another. For instance, *Oklahoma!* is a Western that leans 'way over toward operetta, whereas *Annie Get Your Gun* is a Western that is pure musical comedy. The question again is one of the vernacular: *Oklahoma!* uses realistic Western speech, whereas *Annie* uses tough talk that belongs to New York. *Oklahoma!* tries for cowboy music, whereas *Annie* says it with jazz, Indians to the contrary. Similarly, Frank Loesser's hit *The Most Happy Fella* leans heavily on opera; *Guys and Dolls— by the very same composer—* is the purest musical comedy. *My Fair Lady,* because of its subject matter, is necessarily closer to operetta, whereas *Damn Yankees* is necessarily further from operetta because of *its* subject matter.

But they all qualify, different as they are, for that term "musical comedy" on the grounds of one great unifying factor: they all belong to an art that arises out of American roots, out of our speech, our tempo, our moral attitudes, our way of moving. Out of all this, a new form has been born. Some people claim that it is the forerunner of a new kind of opera; others insist it will never become opera, because it is not art, nor is it meant to be anything but light entertainment. Being a liberal, I can see both sides. We will always have with us the line of gorgeous girls, the star comic, and the razzle-dazzle band in the pit.

But there's more in the wind than that. We are in a historical position now similar to that of the popular musical theater in Germany just before Mozart came along. In 1750, the big attraction was what they called the *Singspiel,* which was the *Annie Get Your Gun* of its day, star comic and all. This popular form took the leap to a work of art through the genius of Mozart. After all, *The Magic Flute* is a *Singspiel;* only it's by Mozart. *

We are in the same position; all we need is for our Mozart to come along. If and when he does, we surely won't get any *Magic Flute;* what we'll get will be a new form, and perhaps "opera" will be the wrong word for it. There must be a more exciting word for such an exciting event. And this event can happen any second. It's almost as though it is our moment in history, as if there is a historical necessity that gives us such a wealth of creative talent at this precise time.

(The telecast concluded with a performance of "Another Opening, Another Show," from Cole Porter's Kiss Me, Kate.*)*

---

* Compare with related ideas in "Whatever Happened to That Great American Symphony?," page 40.

INTRODUCTION
TO MODERN MUSIC

TELECAST: JANUARY 13, 1957

Leonard Bernstein:

Here it is a nice, quiet Sunday evening in January, and we are about to listen to some beautiful music. Immediately, this suggests a pattern: low lights, your favorite chair, a glass of beer, a cigarette, those warm bunny slippers— in short, relaxation. And now the music:

Orchestra, wildly:

Now, don't run away screaming, "Crazy modern music!" It won't bite you. It's only music, and charming music at that, about a little nightingale. This *Song of the Nightingale*, by Stravinsky, was not written to shock, or upset the bourgeoisie, or provoke fist fights. It was written only to charm, to entertain, to be pleasant and touching.

But we do have a certain amount of so-called *avant-garde* music in our modern art which does try to shock and be original for originality's sake. There are certain composers, for example, who are writing for something called the "prepared piano," which involves stuffing the inside of the piano with a variety of paraphernalia, including nuts and bolts, in order to alter the normal piano timbre. The inside of the piano might look a little like this:

Then we have composers who are putting artificial music electronically on tape.

Then there is another type of composition called "unpredictable music," which can be written, for example, for an orchestra of radios.*

Compared with these wildest outposts of experimentation, that bit of Stravinsky's *Song of the Nightingale* seems tame, and more like— well, music. But, still, it's *modern* music.

What makes it modern? And why do so many of you hate what it is that makes it modern? Let's find out. Maybe after you know what it is that you hate, you may hate it less, or at least hate it more intelligently. Or conceivably you may grow to like it, or you can go on hating it as before, which is your democratic right.

But the fact is that a lot of people do dislike modern music. "No," they say, "I can't take all that cacophony and noise. I may

---

* E.g. *Imaginary Landscapes for Twelve Radios* by John Cage, which is scored for radio frequencies and volumes, resulting in chance sounds. This too can sound spooky, nightmarish, or insanely aggressive, depending on what station WXXX and its rivals happen to be broadcasting at any given second. In any case, it's bound to be "modern."

be old-fashioned, but I hate dissonance. It's all so dissonant, and it has no melody. It's a sign of the times, of our machine age, of our neuroses, of the insane tempo of city life, taxi-taxi, wild youth, crime"— all that sort of thing.

But the question they are really asking is: "What has happened to *beauty*, the kind of beauty we associate with Mozart and Chaikovsky?" Have modern composers forgotten beauty? Any modern composer will tell you that his artistic goals are exactly the same as Mozart's and Chaikovsky's were: to write beautiful music. And actually the music he writes, with the exception of things like a symphony for radios, is only a natural extension of all the music that preceded it. Similarly, those great composers of the past who were considered revolutionary in their own time were only extending the scope of the musical tradition *they* inherited.

However, one basic change has occurred, a change which may explain why so many people ask that question, "What has happened to beauty?" This change involves tonality, and to understand it we must first understand what is meant by tonality.

Tonality means simply that quality in music which presents one particular tone as the principal one— called the tonic— while all the other tones are dependent on it.

If you picture a baseball diamond, with home plate as the tonic note, you will immediately see what I mean:

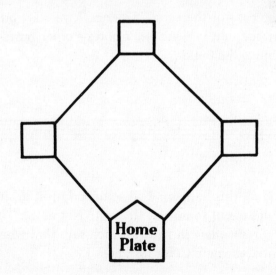

Home Plate

The three bases are notes which are different from, but related to, the tonic home plate. One can run around these bases in order, or one can skip among them arbitrarily; but the point is always to return eventually home, to our tonic home plate.

For example, if we take C as our tonic home plate:

L. B. plays piano:

these other three notes could well be the three bases:

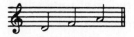

and then we return home again:

Or in the case of the song "America," we start on the tonic and meander through various other notes— other bases— and then return home to the tonic.

How did all this happen? Did somebody just arbitrarily make up these rules about tonic and the rest? Not at all. They arise out of a basic physical law in nature which says that when any one note is sounded, the note C, for instance:

L. B. plays piano:

it is not the *only* tone that is being heard at the moment. This note C is made up of many other tones called overtones, which are sounding at the same time higher and fainter.

Does this surprise you? Well, it's true. And what it means is that every time you hear that low C played, you are also hearing a long series of overtones, whether you know it or not. The first overtone must be again C:

and the second overtone G, a fifth higher than the second C:

then comes C again, a fourth higher:

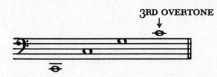

then E, a third higher:

and so on and on, the notes getting progressively closer together, until the human ear can't distinguish them, and so high that the human ear can't detect them:

Just for fun, let's try this simple experiment on the piano, and see if we can hear an isolated overtone. Depress middle C very carefully so as not to let it sound; then sharply strike and quickly release the C an octave below. As soon as the lower C is released, what will you hear? The *upper* C! It seems like magic, because you have really not "struck" this higher C, but the lower one. But what you have done is this: you have released the damper on the upper C-string, which allows it to vibrate sympathetically as the first overtone of the C an octave below. The same experiment can be tried using other overtones of that lower C.

The importance of this experiment is enormous. It means that any note struck will sound forth not only as the note struck, but will contain in addition *all its own* overtones. (Obviously, the lower the note struck, the more overtones will be sounding simultaneously. That is why low notes sound richer than higher ones: they contain more audible overtones.)

Now imagine primitive man and his first musical experience. Obviously, the first music he tried must have been vocal chanting, and that must have all been on one note. Something like this:

---

* Actually, this overtone exists a bit lower than the B-flat on our modern well-tempered piano. It lies in the crack between the A and the B-flat. The same is true of certain others in the series. But to explain why would take a whole other program, about the well-tempered scale.

L. B. sings:

OH   RAIN - GOD   BRING   US   RAIN!

But in singing, or hearing that one note, he was automatically hearing the overtones contained in it; and as his ear sharpened (over how many years!), it was only a matter of time before he became aware of those harmonic (overtone) sounds and began to sing *them* too.

Out of them he made musical patterns. Thus, one might imagine that same prayer for rain advancing from one note to two different notes, once the first overtone had been grasped.

OH   RAIN - GOD   BRING   US   RAIN!

Then once he began to hear the *second* overtone, he might have sung:

OH   RAIN - GOD   BRING   US   RAIN!

And then, with the admission of the next highest overtone, the third:

OH   RAIN - GOD   BRING   US   RAIN!

Musical language would now have had the enormous vocabulary of three different notes, which make up the common triad:

L. B. plays:

— the bread and butter of our musical culture. We have not yet formed a baseball *diamond*, but at least we have a triangle:

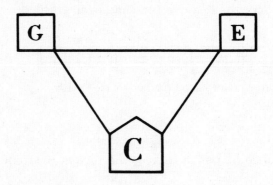

— with the tonic as home plate and the other two notes of the triad as the two bases. Out of this triad many of the melodies we know best have been made, like the "Blue Danube Waltz," for instance:

L. B. plays piano:

or any bugle call at all:

Trumpet:

or the opening theme of the *Eroica* symphony:

Trumpet:

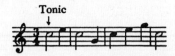

In every case you can hear that one note, and only one, is the main one, or the tonic.

In time there came to be *five* different tones in the language:

— the first five different overtones of the series; and out of them was born a primitive five-note scale— or, as we say in the trade, a pentatonic scale:

This group of notes forms the basis of almost all the folk music of the world. The five black notes of the piano happen to correspond (in a well-tempered way) to this pentatonic scale:

You can actually play folk tunes of almost any ethnic origin by using only black notes; for example, Chinese:

L. B. plays piano:

or Scottish:

or American Indian:

or whatever you wish. In other words, we now have not just a baseball diamond, but a pentagon, with a home plate and *four* bases to run.

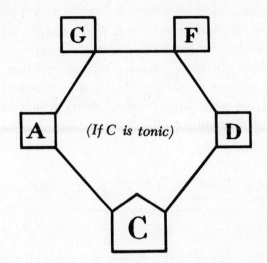

As civilization progressed, more and more overtones were added, so that in the great flowering of Greek culture, for example, scales came into being that contained not five, but *seven* tones. So now our baseball diamond has grown to a heptagon, with home plate and *six* bases to run.

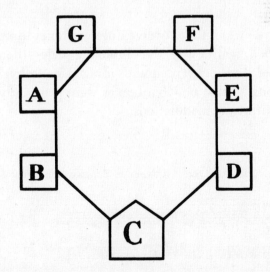

Now, why am I telling you all this? You thought we were talking about modern music, and here we are discussing ancient Greek scales.

But there is method in my madness. I want to help you see the growth of Western music as a *tonal system,* whereby there is always one fundamental note, one tonic center, which is the center to which all other notes are related, whether it is melody or harmony we are dealing with. So that when you consider the music of the past three hundred years which has all of *twelve* notes at its disposal:

you can understand that somewhere among all those twelve tones there has to be a tonal center, a home plate, a point of reference, a point of repose, a focus, a locus, what you wish, but in any case a place to get back to, no matter how skittishly you have been running around those eleven other bases.*

Once we had all these twelve different tones to work with— which are called, by the way, the chromatic scale— the growth of music was thereafter concerned with using them in freer and freer combinations, so that new harmonies were constantly appearing, and more surprising modulations.

* As, for example, in the first theme of Shostakovich's *First Symphony*

That word *modulation* may sound fancy and technical to you, but actually it is rather easy to understand. To modulate means simply to move from one key to another, from one *tonality* to another. For example, I start "The Star-Spangled Banner" in the key of C:

L. B. plays piano:

and suddenly shift to the key of A-flat:

then to B:

and then back to the key of C:

— home plate. I have modulated away from C, and then I have modulated back to it again. Why? For the sake of variety. That's the clue to what was happening in the development of music. Composers had begun to find it boring to stick in one tonality for any length of time, and they naturally began to wander with ever-increasing restlessness from one tonality to another. Before long they had become obsessed with the new possibilities of richness and variety in music. And as each major composer extended this development a little further, the umpires of the music world howled in confusion and anger. "Discords!" cried the critics about Beethoven's *Fifth:*

Piano:

"Discords to shatter the least sensitive ear," they said. And of a Chopin mazurka:

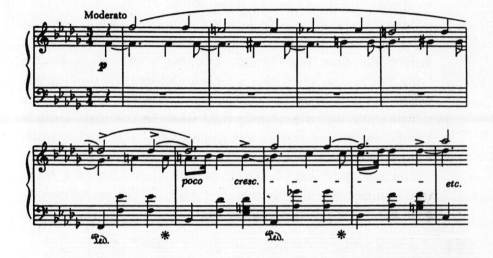

they said, "Ear-rending dissonances." And of Brahms's *Second Symphony* it was said: "It would appear as though Brahms might afford occasionally to put a little more melody into his work— just a little now and then, for a change.":

Piano:

"A little more melody," indeed!

But that's exactly the cry we hear today about contemporary music: there's no melody, and it's so dissonant! Well, it's high time we decided what we mean by these words.

Take melody. What is it, anyway? A melody is a succession of different tones, so organized as to produce a meaningful and memorable effect. But meaning in music is after all an elusive thing. All we can say is that a meaningful series of tones is one which moves us in one way or another, one which seems to have artistic truth. But, if Keats was right when he said that "Truth is beauty" and vice versa, then any melody which strikes us as artistically true must be beautiful.

The melody of that Chopin mazurka we heard before is beautiful— nobody would deny that. But what of this famous melody from Beethoven's *Seventh Symphony?*

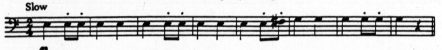

Is that a beautiful melody? It's practically all on one note! Yet the whole world says it's beautiful! Well, it isn't— that is, the melody by *itself* isn't. But it's part of a great truth— a meaningful, artistic concept:

Orchestra:

So what people mean by a beautiful melody isn't a melody at all, but a *tune,* and that's a very different word. This tune of Offenbach's, for example, is heavenly:

L. B. plays piano:

but you wouldn't ever put it in the same class with Beethoven as far as *beauty* is concerned, even though it's a much prettier tune than that Johnny-One-Note by Beethoven. So you see that melody is a highly relative idea. And when you say that you don't like a modern piece because it lacks melody, watch out. That's probably not what you mean at all.

O.K., what's dissonance? A much maligned word, used just as loosely as "melody" to explain musical displeasure. But actually, the music you love most couldn't exist without dissonance. Dissonance is one of the very foundations of musical expression, since a dissonant note (which means a note that doesn't belong in any given chord) will always be the most expressive note in that chord precisely *because* it doesn't belong.

For example, take the famous melody from Chaikovsky's *Romeo and Juliet.*

It actually begins on a fierce dissonance:

Orchestra:

What a tension it creates:

— and what a sense of pleasurable relief when it resolves:

So you see that dissonance is also relative, and that its development, along with such things as modulation and new harmonies, has given music constantly greater and greater expressive power.

By the time Richard Wagner came along with his opera *Tristan and Isolde,* this expressivity had hit an all-time high. Somehow, in the very first few bars of *Tristan,* Wagner had already created a music that was so dissonant, so expressive, so chromatic, so wandering in its modulations from key to key that the poor listener had almost lost his tonal bearings. He didn't know where he was; he was hard put to it to find a tonic home plate. Where are we in this music? We are suspended in some highly perfumed region, floating around in an atmosphere of unconsummated desire. Look at this melody: it yearns upward:

L. B. plays piano:

and then hits a great tension:

and then resolves:

but it resolves only to another unresolved chord. Pause. Then
again it tries yet higher:

and again the stab of desire:

and again the unfulfilled resolution:

Pause, while we are again suspended, and then still higher:

and yet another stab:

and again we resolve to no resolution:

Where are we? We are adrift in a sea of indefinite tonality.

You see, these twelve tones have now begun to acquire an almost equal importance. They are living in a democratic anarchy, instead of in an organized society governed by one definite tonic note, as had always been the case with Bach, Beethoven and Brahms. And so the legacy that Wagner left the world was one of general pandemonium.

What would you have done if you had been a poor, benighted, post-Wagnerian composer? You'd have been in a tight spot, because there didn't seem to be anything left to write. Tonal procedures had become so free there didn't even seem to be any freedoms left to take. Nothing was amazing any more after *Tristan and ·Isolde.*

The reactions to this terrible and wonderful moment in music were various. But it is these reactions that constitute, for better or for worse, what we know today as modern music.

For out of this crisis came a great split, a split that has the musical world divided even to this day, controversy over whether tonality is valid at all any more. All twentieth-century composers can thus be divided into two camps: the atonalists, who believe

tonality to be a dead duck, as against all the others, who are strug-
gling to preserve tonality at all costs.

Let's first take a brief look at that strange, esoteric world of
atonality. It all began around 1910 with a genius named Arnold
Schoenberg. Schoenberg started in the Wagner tradition, solidly
enough entrenched in *Tristan*. His first well-known work, written
at the age of twenty-five, was a string sextet called *Verklaerte
Nacht,* or *Transfigured Night,* in which he was actually out-
Wagnering Wagner. As you listen to it with all its Wagnerian pain
and longing, see if you can also hear the Wagnerian tonalities
tearing at the seams: *

String Sextet:

Beautiful stuff, but Schoenberg was in a blind alley. He had
stretched tonality to such a point of agony that he couldn't stretch
any more without actually tearing it to pieces. So tear it he did,
and destroyed it entirely. And out came atonal music— music
composed with no sense of key at all, no home plate, no bases to
run, just music using the twelve tones. It sounded like this:

String Quartet:

OP. 30, NO. 3—MVT. II.*

Can you see that this had to be the next step after *Verklaerte Nacht?* Actually, the two pieces are very much alike, only the first is tonal and the second is atonal. But they are both made out of the same piece of tissue, with the same agonized leaps and hysterical tensions. All this was psychologically right in line with the Vienna of Schoenberg's time, that same middle-European factory of the unconscious that produced Freud and expressionistic painting and nightmare poetry.

Out of this nightmare world, in 1912, came that weird song cycle, Schoenberg's *Pierrot Lunaire.* This is a piece which never fails to move and impress me, but always leaves me feeling a little bit sick. This is only just, since sickness is what it's about— moon-sickness. Somewhere in the middle of this piece you have a great desire to run and open a window, breathe in a lungful of healthy, clean air. But after all, that is the measure of its success. Here is one of the songs, accompanied only by a flute. The singer doesn't exactly sing, but indulges in a sort of declamation called *Sprechtstimme,* which is part singing, part speaking, part moaning. This song is aptly called "The Sick Moon": **

Voice and flute:

This is the sound of free atonality. But Schoenberg, being culturally of the German tradition, could never be content with such a lawless procedure. A German has to have a system. And so Schoenberg substituted for the old discarded tonal system a brand-new one for writing atonal music, which is known as the twelve-tone system, and which guarantees, or your money back, that you will compose atonal music with no danger of anything resembling a key creeping in. In essence, it's simple. You take the twelve notes of the chromatic scale:

and arrange them in any arbitrary order, at will. This is called a tone-row, and it might sound like this:

L. B. plays piano:

The tone-row is now used, *instead* of a scale, as the basis of any given movement or piece. You have to know how to manipulate these tone rows contrapuntally back and forth, inside out, upside down. It can become very complex. There's not even a tonic home plate to slide into.

Question one: Is this kind of music denying a basic law of nature when it denies tonality?

Question two: Is the human ear equipped to take it all in?

And question three: If the human ear can take it in, will the heart be moved?

Many people feel that it remained for Schoenberg's great disciple Alban Berg to take the twelve-tone system and, so to speak, humanize it, in such noble works as his *Violin Concerto*, his great opera *Wozzeck*, and his *Lyric Suite* for string quartet. Listen to this passionate section of the third movement of the *Lyric Suite*, in which you can hear those abnormally wide leaps and stretches which are almost a trademark of atonal music:*

Quartet:

Lyric Suite, Berg, Alban; copyright 1927 by Universal Edition. Copyright renewed. All rights reserved. Used by permission of European American Music Distributors Corporation, sole U.S. and Canadian agent for Universal Edition.

And, finally, that wonderful passage from the last movement of
the *Lyric Suite*, which introduces, of all things, a direct quote
from *Tristan and Isolde*, note for note:

Quartet:

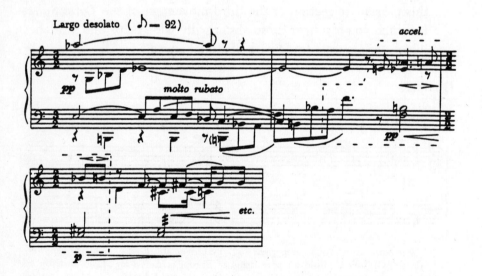

This was, of course, intended deliberately as a quote by way of tribute. But in the quote we see clearly the source from which this great whole atonal river has flowed.

Meanwhile, back at home plate, tonal composers had not given up. Debussy, for all his ambivalent efforts to weaken tonality (in the form of whole-tone scales, arbitrary movement of tonal centers, etc.), actually did more to preserve tonality than to destroy it. His important and influential experiments in atonalism succeeded more in providing new atmospheres in which tonality could exist than in rendering tonality obsolete. Debussy is pure middle ground; and today his music has taken its place in history: it no longer is the adventure it once was. For example, what is there more comfortable and acceptable to the average modern ear than *The Afternoon of a Faun?*

Flute:

It was now a question of saving tonality by giving it a new look, and this Debussy did by treating it with all the devices of French impressionism.

You see, the musical center of the world was now shifting to Paris, away from Wagner and the whole overblown German romantic movement he represented. A group had begun to form in Paris around the pioneering figure of Erik Satie, who answered that movement by simply refusing to be "grand." He would write only the simplest little music, a little tune with a little accompaniment, like this dispassionate *Gymnopédie* (No. 3), which is still played and loved:

L. B. plays piano:

How fresh this must have sounded in 1888 against that heavy German background! This was Satie's way of saving tonality. By the turn of the century, Satie had become a powerful influence on Debussy, Ravel, Milhaud and other great French composers who learned this new simplicity and objectivity at his knee.

Objectivity— that was the keynote. It cleared the air, gave new tone to music, made it leaner and more muscular and less— well, Wagnerian. It also brought out the sense of humor in music which was a long-neglected item. But it's only natural that a reaction against German romanticism should involve a certain amount of poking fun and satire. So there grew up a school of "ha-ha" music in which funny wrong notes became a specialty— like that early Shostakovich *Polka* (from the *Golden Age* ballet) containing deliberate wrong notes and other bumptious surprises designed to make the audience laugh:

Orchestra:

Perhaps a more serious aspect of this new objectivity can be found in the bareness of texture which about then began to inhabit music. There was a general spring-cleaning of all sound, getting rid of all those romantic old cobwebs, as can be heard in this much later Shostakovich work, his *Fifth Symphony:*

Orchestra:

This whole objective spirit, with its simplicity, its clarity, its dry humor, its thin textures and all the rest, led naturally to a movement called neo-classicism, which looked for inspiration back to the eighteenth century, to Bach, Haydn and Mozart, before music had been sugared up by romanticism. The neo-classic call to arms was issued by Stravinsky in 1923, in Paris, in the form of a harmless little *Octet for Wind Instruments*, which was clear, precise, dry, and full of Bach:

Orchestra:

Back to Bach, but oh, so different. And in that difference lies the key to modern tonal music. The difference consists in all the various ways that have been used to preserve old-fashioned tonality by making it sound fresh and new and, excuse the expression, modern.

What are these ways? Well, first of all there was the mass return to basic musical materials like the good old scales, in order to get away from that twelve-tone nightmare. Forget the chromatic scale for a while, they said. Let's see if there's life in the old seven-note, or diatonic, scale. And so out came works like Copland's *Appalachian Spring,* which is as diatonic as a nursery rhyme:

Orchestra:

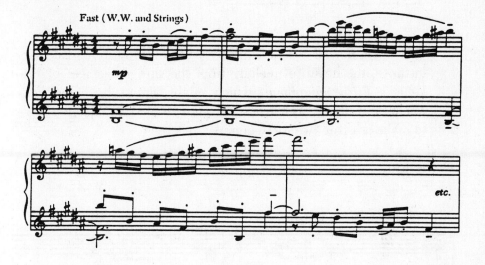

Sometimes composers went back farther, to the old Greek scales. And sometimes even farther back to that primitive pentatonic scale (you remember those five black notes?):

All this reinvestigation of the old scales was bound up, of course, with a new interest in melody, an interest that had somehow gotten lost in the post-Wagnerian woods. A modern symphony like Roy Harris' *Third* can thus open with a stream of melody that is as rich and pure of line as an old Gregorian chant. But it's just that archaic quality that makes it sound clean and modern, compared with the old, fat plushness of Wagner.

Orchestra:

Of course, not all our melodic writing is that austere. Take, for instance, the beautiful melody from the slow movement of Prokofieff's *Fifth Symphony*, which might almost be called neoromantic in flavor. Yet it has just enough of that objective spirit to make it a true twentieth-century melody:

Orchestra:

This is tonality made fresh and young and beautiful again.

But perhaps the chief way to rejuvenate tonality is through a much freer use of our old friend dissonance. For example, picture two different melodies going along simultaneously in counterpoint. At certain points along the route there must inevitably be clashes.

For example, I might play you "America" with one hand and "The Star-Spangled Banner" with the other at the same time, and you would get something that inevitably clashes in places, like this:

L. B. plays piano:

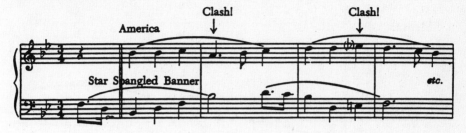

Now, if you want to be conventional, you have to fix one tune or the other in order to avoid clashes, like this:

But if you want to be modern, it's simple: just don't fix it. Leave all the dissonant clashes in.

Of course, this procedure is ridiculously oversimplified. Actually, modern dissonant counterpoint demands technical handling and sensitive selection fully as much as old "consonant" counterpoint does; the only difference is that the use of dissonance is far freer and no longer subject to the ancient rules of preparation and resolution. This would account for that strange sound at the beginning of Hindemith's *Concert Music for Strings and Brass,* for example, where the brass is playing a perfectly normal melody:*

Brass:

---

* *Concert Music for String Orchestra and Brass*. Op. 50, Hindemith, Paul; Copyright © 1931 B. Schott's Soehne, Mainz; copyright renewed. All rights reserved. Used by permission of European American Music Distributors Corporation, sole U.S. and Canadian agent for B. Schott's Soehne, Mainz.

and the strings are playing a fairly normal series of figurations:

Strings:

Each one is perfectly fine by itself; but together:

Orchestra:

See? Modern music.

But these different clashes can be exciting; and one of the most exciting aspects of dissonance is a device called bitonality, which means, of course, the use of two tonalities at the same time. For example, if I should play the tune of the "Blue Danube Waltz" in one key:

and the accompaniment in another:

I would have a simple example of bitonal art:

See? Again, modern music.

Bitonality has always been a favorite device of Stravinsky.

Much of his *Petrouchka*, for example, derives its bite and freshness from this simple method. You remember those arresting
trumpet calls at the end? Their effectiveness comes from the same
bitonal procedure: one trumpet plays a C-major flourish:

Trumpet I:

and the other trumpet flourishes in F-sharp major:

Trumpet II:

Together they make that *"Petrouchka* sound."

Trumpets I and II:

And what about rhythm? Modern composers have found this, of
all musical areas, the least explored and exploited by the great
composers of the past. The German tradition has presented rhythm
in a fairly undeveloped way: square, symmetrical and regular:

Orchestra:

A modern Haydn might easily do the opposite and make it asymmetrical and irregular. Something like this:

L. B. plays piano:

— or any number of other types of rhythmic distortion.

There are countless new ways to use rhythm— through syncopation, changing meters, displaced accents, cross-rhythms, and all the rest. The best example of all this is Stravinsky's *Rite of Spring*, which once and for all took the shackles off rhythm. For example, consider these barbaric displaced accents:

Orchestra:

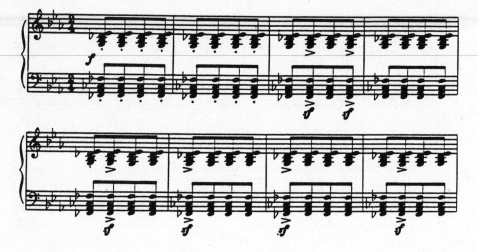

Much of this new interest in rhythm arises from the twentieth-century composer's fascination with jazz. Jazz has not only bequeathed new rhythms to music, but also it has taught composers the handling of cross-rhythms.* Let me give you a simple example. I'm sure you all remember an old Gershwin tune called "Fidgety Feet" that has in the left hand a simple 4/4 bass:

L. B. plays piano:

while the right hand has phrases in 3/4 time!

---

* I.e., more than one metrical pattern at a time.

Together the two hands make a charming interplay:

This simple principle has been extended by the modern composer into some pretty terrifying complexity. Listen to this section of Copland's *El Salón Mexico,* where you can hear all the rhythmic aberrations in the book, and all in terms of simple Mexican folk music:

Orchestra:

You see what exciting stuff that is?

And a lot of the fun and excitement is provided by the composer's constant search for new colors, new instruments, new exciting instrumental combinations. It's always that new sound that he's after, a twentieth-century sound. The trick is to get away from the standard symphony-orchestra sound that the Germans had built into such a great monument. Milhaud invented a knockout of a sonority for his ballet *The Creation of the World,* which is kind of like the sound of a long-hair Dixieland band:

Orchestra:

A brand-new sound. Or take these weird night-sounds that come from Bartók's *Music for Strings, Percussion and Celesta:*

Orchestra:

I could cite you dozens of others.

So you see how, with new sounds, new sonorities, new textures, dissonances, harmonies, rhythms, and that new objective approach, a great modern composer can use the same old-fashioned notes that music has always used, and use them in a fresh way. And I guess that's what people mean by a composer's "having something to say." If he has something to say, then perhaps he doesn't have to resort to the twelve-tone system of Schoenberg for guaranteed originality. Perhaps there's life in the old tonal boy yet.

Take the very last chord of Stravinsky's *Symphony of Psalms*, a simple old home-plate tonic triad in C-major, which Stravinsky spaces and orchestrates like this:

Orchestra:

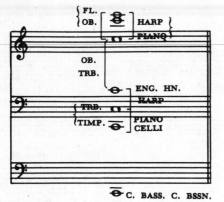

C. BASS. C. BSSN.

What makes this sound so fresh? First, that Stravinsky leaves out
the fifth of the triad (G); second, that he uses the tonic root (C)
for the entire chord, except for the flute and oboe tone (E) at the
very top. The bareness of this spacing allows the natural overtones
to sound in the wide-open spaces, suggestively replacing the *real*
sounds that would have thickened up a more romantic version of
the chord. And even that little E on the top sounds like an overtone. It is as though the chord were nothing but a series of C's
with their natural overtones filling in the gaps, making a "chord"
that is pure, cool, rarefied, exalted— perhaps the purest single
orchestral chord ever heard on this earth. There you have it:
basic musical material made new by genius.

And so we have seen a picture of modern music divided into
two camps, tonal and atonal, with Stravinsky and Schoenberg as
the top heap-big chiefs. In the last few years, we have been surprised to find that the two camps have been coming closer together. Stravinsky has become deeply interested in the twelve-tone
technique, and his latest music shows it. This is also true of many
other tonal composers. On the other hand, many atonal composers
are becoming more tonal. In both cases, they are engaged in the
same struggle for new beauty. Perhaps this synthesis points the
direction for the future of modern music, and toward a new kind
of beauty.

But think of the miracle that we, now in the sixth decade of the twentieth century, have so much beauty in our music. *That's* the wonder: not that we don't have a Beethoven or a Chopin in our time. What would we do with them if we had them? They have given us their glorious works; now it is for our contemporary artists to give us theirs. Don't worry about finding it hard to absorb or accept. You're absorbing new art all the time, much more than you may consciously realize. The innovations of James Joyce are to be found in some paperbacked novel you may buy for a quarter in the drugstore. Or when you are looking at a chewing-gum advertisement on the bus, you may be admiring some version of Mondrian or Miró. And while you're watching a play on television, the background music may be by Bartók. If you go to the movies, you are most likely going to hear modern music in the score. How many of you saw a recent film called *The Cobweb*? And how many of you realized, as you were watching the divine Lauren Bacall, that there was a frankly atonal score going on* — about an hour of atonal music?

Well, it's only a step from *The Cobweb* to the concert hall, from Wrigley's gum to the Modern Museum, from the drugstore novel to *Ulysses*.

Be glad for modern art. And modern music is your music.

* By Leonard Rosenman.

THE MUSIC OF
JOHANN
SEBASTIAN
BACH

TELECAST: MARCH 31, 1957

Chorus and orchestra:

Leonard Bernstein:

> BACH!
>
> A colossal syllable, one which makes composers tremble, brings performers to their knees, beatifies the Bach-lover, and apparently bores the daylights out of everyone else. How can this be? How can vibrant, thrilling music like that bore anyone? Still, it's true; many of you find Bach dull. No— don't deny it; there's nothing to be ashamed of, because the boredom comes only from the fact that it's not very easy music to know, and you must know it to love it. Maybe the trouble is that you don't get a chance to know it; you don't hear much Bach. After all, to hear Bach you have to go to certain churches faithfully, or to certain very special little concerts.
>
> How many of you have experienced the simple strength of a

---

* *from: Magnificat (end of No. 7— "Fecit potentiam")*

237

Bach chorale? How many of you know the power and majesty of his organ music? Have you heard the charm and delicacy of his flute music? Have you experienced the singing warmth of Bach's melodies? How often have you shared Bach's joyful celebration of God, as in the *Magnificat?*

Chorus:

What drive, what life! And you've probably never heard it.

But the real trouble is that even if you *have* heard it, it's still difficult music to know.

And knowing Bach doesn't mean knowing that he died in Leipzig in 1750 and that he had two wives and twenty-one children. It means knowing the *music,* and that's the tough job we've set ourselves tonight. And that's also the challenge, because once you do get to know Bach well enough to love him, you will love him more than any other composer. I know this because I went through the same process myself.

For me, Bach meant very little until I was seventeen or so and began to study the *Saint Matthew Passion.* Before that, Bach had meant only some pretty monotonous stuff I sometimes heard at concerts and on the radio, plus some piano pieces I was given to practice. There were exceptions, of course. A piece like the *Chromatic Fantasy* used to excite me greatly, because of its quality of improvisation and its virtuoso impact:

L. B. at piano:

And I can remember being deeply moved by the slow movement of the *Italian Concerto,* with its long, mournful line of pure Italian melody:

Piano:

Why did these pieces touch me, when most of Bach's music didn't? It was because of their immediacy. They were instantly comprehensible to me as expressions of joy, or grief, or power, whereas the mainstream of Bach's work seemed to be nothing but endless pages of sixteenth-notes, chugging along like a train:

Piano:

FUGUE IN A-MINOR

and any emotion contained in it was hardly discernible to me; it seemed more like motion than emotion.

I remember trying to find ways of playing such music that would make it more exciting— like giving it rhythmic distortions, which I thought was giving it warmth:

Piano:

Or I would try to turn it into a whirlwind of virtuosity and lightness:

Or I would try to make it sound like a great dynamic eruption:

All these ways were, of course, dead wrong, because they were only artificially covering up what seemed a basic dullness. But I was soon to learn that there are great beauties hidden in this music; only they are not so immediate as we expect them to be. They lie beneath the surface. But because they do, they don't rub off so easily; they last and last.

Why is Bach's music less immediate than, say, that of Brahms or Chaikovsky? Perhaps the main reason is that his music is not *obviously* dramatic. We have been so spoiled by music written since Bach's time, which is essentially dramatic in nature, that we have come to expect drama of one sort or another in music, and we're disappointed and bored when we don't see it.

Now, what makes music dramatic anyway? Contrast— and I mean contrast as a principle of composition, the principle of duality, of two themes, two contrasting ideas or emotions within a single movement.

It is in the music written *since* Bach that the dualistic principle has flourished. Think of almost any Beethoven symphony— say, the *Eroica*. The first theme is masculine in quality:

L. B. at piano:

the second theme is feminine:

Or take Rachmaninoff's *Second Piano Concerto*. The first theme is aggressive and agitated:

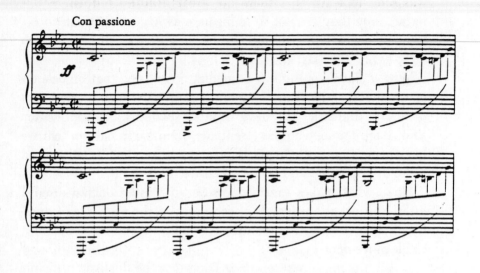

while the second is lyrical and reposeful.

And there is always the further contrast of tonalities; the first theme of the Rachmaninoff, for example, is in C-minor and the second in E-flat major.

Contrast makes drama— black against white, good against evil, day and night, grief and joy. Bach represented the last stand *against* the dualistic concept. Any single movement is always concerned with one single idea. Bach clung to the older concept of one thing at a time— grief *or* joy, day *or* night— which is certainly as valid a concept as the other. Only we've been spoiled; and so, to enjoy Bach, we must reorient ourselves and learn to expect music that is always about one thing at a time. Once the theme is stated at the beginning, the main event is over. The rest of the movement will be a constant elaboration, reiteration, and discussion of that main event, just as the architecture of a bridge grows inevitably out of one initial arch.

When you listen to the opening bars of the *Fifth Brandenburg Concerto*, I think you'll see what I mean:

Chamber orchestra:

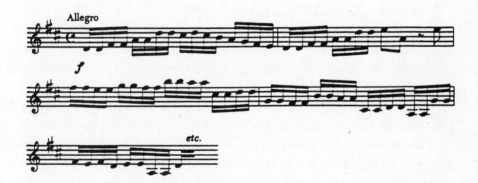

This is the arch; the rest of the bridge follows logically and inevitably.

On and on it goes, in the same way, spinning out those wonderful long lines. But if you're expecting any change in mood, a sudden slowing down or a yielding to sentimental lyricism— contrast, in other words— you're not going to get it. Contrast is there all right, but it's restricted to loud and soft, or key changes, or different instrumental groupings, but the *dramatic* contrast of themes is *not* there.

We have here music based on *one* chain of related themes, which are treated, developed, and investigated to the hilt. This is known as the argumentative technique, the technique of taking one subject and discussing it fully, which sounds, offhand, rather intellectual— and I suppose it is. But whoever said that music had to be easy to be beautiful? Let's just admit it's complex, pull in our belts, take a deep breath and get to know Bach on his own terms.

The first term we already know: the argumentative or nondramatic technique. Now for the second term, that frightening bugaboo, counterpoint.

Why are people so scared of this word? When "counterpoint" is mentioned, or, even worse, when its adjectival cousin "contrapuntal" is mentioned, people throw up their hands. "Don't bother me with all that counterpoint stuff. I don't get it. Give me a good simple melody." Well, there's nothing to be scared of. Counterpoint *is* melody, only accompanied by one or more additional melodies, running along at the same time.

You may recall that on another *Omnibus* program* I played "The Star-Spangled Banner" with my left hand and "America" with my right, with resulting dissonant clashes. Out of this consideration arises the very fine art of counterpoint, the art which fixes rules for making two or more melodic lines go well together. As you saw, by changing a few notes in one of the lines I made those two tunes fit together. Of course it meant that "America" was no longer quite the same tune, but it made good counterpoint.

But why counterpoint anyway? Why complicate matters? The theory is that two melodies at once must be twice as interesting as one. By the same token, I suppose, six melodies going on at once are six times as interesting, and six times harder to write. *And,* I admit, six times harder to listen to.

But again, it's only a question of our having been spoiled by the music we hear most of the time, music which emphasizes har-

---

* See "Introduction to Modern Music," page 180.

mony instead of counterpoint. In other words, we are used to hearing a melody on top, with chords supporting it underneath like pillars— melody and harmony, a tune and its accompaniment:

Orchestra:

Franck, *SYMPHONY IN D-MINOR*

That's our basic idea of music, only because in the last two hundred years or so music has grown in that direction.

But before that, people used to listen to music differently. The ear was conditioned to hear *lines*, simultaneous melodic lines, rather than chords. That was the natural way of music, strange though it seems to us. Counterpoint came before harmony, which is a comparatively recent phenomenon. Actually, all primitive music, like Oriental folk music today, is made of *lines*, just as present-day jazz is also primarily involved with line. That's why jazzmen idolize Bach. For them, he is the great model for the continuously running melody, and this is natural, because Bach and the jazz player both feel music in terms of line— that is, horizontally.

Melody is a horizontal idea of music, flowing along through time in a linear way:

L. B. at piano:

ART OF THE FUGUE (Contrapunctus II)

and so is counterpoint, which is an abundance of horizontal melodies flowing at once, as in this Bach fugue:

String quartet:

Here are four melodic lines at once. But there's another way of looking at it. At any given moment, we can suddenly stop the music:

And what do we have? Four different notes sounding simultaneously, giving us a chord, a vertical sound. This vertical sound is harmony:

L. B. at piano:

— the concept of chords, those pillars that hold up a melody, as in the Bach chorale *Ach, wie nichtig! Ach, wie flüchtig!*:

Chorus:

This is vertical music. But even here there is something horizontal going on. The melody in the soprano is, naturally, horizontal to begin with. But any of the three accompanying voices— alto, tenor or bass— is also singing a linear melody of its own. Here, for instance, is the horizontal line that the bass sings:

Basses:

Ach,   wie   nich - tig   Ach,   wie   flüch - tig

What I hope you're beginning to see is that harmony and counterpoint are interactive, and that there is something of each involved in the other. I have been warned that this is too subtle a point for the nonmusician to grasp, but I don't believe it. And this point is most exciting, because it is the key to Bach's style. Bach fuses the vertical and the horizontal in so marvelous a way that you can never say of any piece of his, "This is only counterpoint," or "This is only harmony." He fashions a kind of sublime crossword puzzle in which the notes of the across "words" and the down "words" are interdependent, where everything checks and all the answers are right.

Now let's apply what we know of Bach's technique to some of his music and begin to solve the crossword puzzle. Starting with his simplest music, the chorale, or Lutheran hymn, we find a familiar, measured melody, easy enough for a whole congregation to remember and be able to sing in church, with harmony supporting it. Bach harmonized hundreds of these chorales, for soprano, alto, tenor and bass, like the one we just saw. On the theory that all four types of voices were to be found in any congregation, and that the members of the congregation could read music, it was hoped that the chorales could be sung in church, harmony and all. Otherwise, the congregation simply sang the soprano part, or the tune.

Everybody knew the tunes, after all. They were mostly popular songs. You see, the Lutheran church had been hungry for music that the worshipers themselves could sing, in contradistinction to the Catholic service, where all the singing was done by the officiating clergy and choir. And so the Protestant movement had grabbed up all kinds of melodies from all over the place: love songs, march tunes, even barroom ballads, songs that crossed the German border from France or Italy. All were eagerly taken up and made into hymns.

For example, take one of the most popular chorale melodies: "O Lamb of God, Most Holy":

L. B. sings:

O　Lamb of God most ho - ly, who on the Cross did lan - guish

Doesn't that sound suspiciously like "Twinkle, Twinkle, Little Star"?:

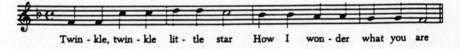

Twin - kle, twin - kle lit - tle star　How I　won - der what you are

As a matter of fact, this tune was a popular folk song of the time, known by the French title *"Ah, Vous Dirai-je, Maman."*

Boys' choir:

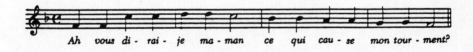

Ah　vous di - rai - je　ma - man　ce　qui cau - se　mon tour - ment?

The chorale tune is different, but it has the same general shape:

Boys' choir:

Bach would take a tune like this, give it to the sopranos, and add harmony in three additional parts; but each of those three parts makes a melodic line that is in itself beautiful and interesting. That is the horizontal aspect of this vertical music. When you listen to this chorale as Bach harmonized it, you'll see what I mean:

Full chorus:

Now you can clearly hear the tune on top, sung by the sopranos. But what's going on underneath? Well, the altos have been singing:

Altos:

The tenors have this phrase:

Tenors:

And the basses sing:

Basses:

We see that each voice has its own horizontal interest, its own melodic beauty. That's why the four voices together produce music that is so profoundly engaging and rich, in spite of its great simplicity.

Rich as the chorale is, Bach took it and developed it into something even richer, called the chorale-prelude. A chorale-prelude is simply a short piece of continuous texture, within which, from time to time, appear the separate phrases of a chorale melody. The chorale-prelude is like a smoothly flowing river whose course is dotted with islands. The river is the main musical material, while the islands are the phrases of the chorale, isolated one from the other. That is where the counterpoint comes in, land and water together. For example, take the chorale tune: "Jesu, Joy of Man's Desiring":

Chorus:

Out of this Bach builds a chorale-prelude for organ. But we don't hear the tune right off. First the river begins its tranquil flow, a melodic line entirely different from the chorale tune, but vaguely related to it:

Organ:

Then the first island approaches, the first phrase of the chorale; and the river goes placidly on:

And now the second island, with the stream continuing simultaneously alongside it:

etc.

The counterpoint is exquisite, so limpid and expressive of the meaning of the chorale. But the counterpoint is born of harmony, the harmony of the chorale tune itself. So again we find harmony and counterpoint inextricably woven together.

From here, Bach takes counterpoint into even more complex regions where dwell the high-bred races of canons and fugues. You all know what a canon is: a device of imitation by one melodic line of another, just as we know it from the simplest rounds we all sang as kids— *"Frère Jacques,"* "Three Blind Mice" and so on. In a canon, as in a round, one voice always begins alone. Let's say I begin with "Row, row, row your boat, gently down the stream"; now you will come in singing the same thing, while I go on to "Merrily, merrily," etc., and there we have the beginning of a canon.

Now, when Bach writes a canon, no matter how complex the counterpoint gets, we can always feel a harmonic structure holding it up. For instance, this Two Part Invention begins canonically. The right hand plays a two-bar phrase, and the left hand comes in later with an exact imitation:

L. B. plays piano:

But, as if by magic, Bach picks notes which not only go together
in wonderful counterpoint, but also manage to produce harmony,
even though there isn't a chord to be seen. Thus these two simple
lines combine to produce the greatest possible *harmonic* strength.
With only two notes at a time, Bach is able to give us a clear impression of harmony so that the listener is never lost between two
separate melodic lines. The implied harmony holds it all together.

The canon leads us naturally to the ultimate expression of
counterpoint— the fugue— which in Bach's hands became a form
so mighty that no composer has ever been able to equal it since.
To analyze the structure of a fugue would be a whole other program, if not a course in a conservatory. But we don't have to be
fugue experts to love Bach. All we have to know, really, is that
the fugue grows out of the canon, and then goes off on tangents,
and episodes, and developments, to become a new, exciting and
complex form.

But even in that maze of counterpoint, Bach saves the situation
by fusing his counterpoint with harmony, so that you are never
in the position of having to follow four separate melodies at once,
like trying to keep up with four telephone conversations. Harmony unites the voices and makes them come together in a single
entity.

Now we're beginning to have some idea of what Bach is about.
The chorale, the chorale-prelude, the canon and the fugue are
the four corners of Bach's musical world. Armed with our knowledge of these, plus our newfound ability to listen horizontally and
vertically at the same time, we are ready for any of Bach's works.
We are going to examine the opening chorus of the *Saint Matthew
Passion*, that glorious work that started me off on my own private
passion for Bach. Complicated as it is, there is nothing in this

chorus that we cannot now understand. It is simply a chorale-
prelude, a river with islands, just like the one we heard before.
Only this chorale-prelude is sung, and the river is no longer tranquil, but churning and heaving.

Orchestra:

This is the orchestral introduction which sets the mood of suffering and pain, preparing for the entrance of the chorus which will sing the agonized sorrow of the faithful at the moment of crucifixion. And this is all done in imitation, in canon. "Come ye Daughters, share my anguish," sing the basses, and they are answered in canon a fifth higher by the tenors:

Men sing:

All this time, the female voices are singing a counter-canon of their own:

Women sing:

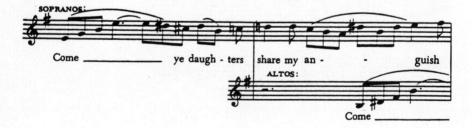

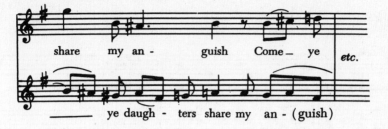

The resulting richness of all the parts, with the orchestra throbbing beneath, is incomparable.

Full orchestra and chorale:

Full orchestra and chorale:

Then suddenly the chorus breaks into two antiphonal choruses. "See Him!" cries the first one. "Whom?" asks the second. And the first answers: "The Bridegroom see. See Him!" "How?" "So like a Lamb." And then over and against all this questioning and answering and throbbing, the voices of a boys' choir sing out the chorale tune, "O Lamb of God Most Holy," piercing through the worldly pain with the icy-clear truth of redemption:

Boys' choir:

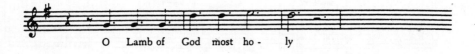

The contrapuntal combination of the three different choruses is thrilling. There is nothing like it in all music:

Full chorus:

Who ever said Bach was undramatic? In this chorus, before the narrator has even begun to tell the story, the drama is already laid before us as tellingly as in the opening of a Greek tragedy. For Bach, nothing could exceed in pity, terror or exaltation the simple story of Christ and the wonder of man's relation to Him. And it is here, in the drama of Christianity, that Bach's dramatic genius burns most brightly.

For example, in the *Saint Matthew Passion,* the events of the Passion Play are sung by a solo tenor in the barest recitative style, accompanied only by a harpsichord, cello and bass. But when the voice of Jesus is heard, even in the recitative passages, the strings enter and surround it with glowing chords, which have often been compared to a halo. Here is such a recitative section, describing the scene of the Last Supper, where Jesus tells his disciples that one of them will betray him— and listen for that halo:

Then there follows one of the most dramatic moments of the whole work, as the disciples' voices tumble over one another in the fearful, anxious question: "Lord, is it I?" Here is a pure dramatic use of counterpoint which makes the scene as real as if it were being acted. Again, Bach the nondramatist turns out to be the superdramatist of them all:

Chorus:

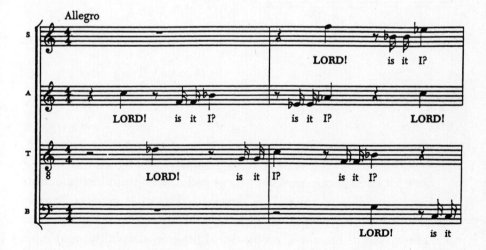

There is a fascinating sidelight to this little chorus. It turns out that the phrase "Lord, is it I?" is repeated exactly eleven times, once for each of the disciples except Judas, who is understandably silent. But this is not only a dramatic device. It reflects Bach's tremendous preoccupation with numbers as symbols. Bach was a mystic, for all his plain, provincial, Lutheran simplicity; and one aspect of this mysticism was his interest in numerology. He was

fond of that Talmudic trick of substituting numbers for letters of
the alphabet and deriving mystical conclusions from the results.

For example, on the principle that A equals 1, B equals 2, etc.,
the name of Bach adds up to 14. For him, this became a mystic
number. The first digit, 1, is the most holy of all numbers, and the
second, 4, represents the four gospels. Furthermore, 1 subtracted
from 4 is 3, the Trinity. 1 and 4 added are 5, the five books of
Moses. The factors of 14 are 2 and 7, both ancient mystic symbols.
But, luckiest of all, the whole name of Johann Sebastian Bach
adds up to 41 (in the old German alphabet), which is the exact
inversion of 14 (the sum of B-A-C-H); and that, to a contrapuntal
mind, must have been a miraculous sign. In fact, in the very last
piece he wrote before he died (the chorale-fantasia *Vor deinen
Thron tret' ich allhier),* the first phrase contains exactly 14 notes,
and the whole melody contains 41 notes.

This almost naïve mystic streak shows up all through the *Passion,* in the form of musical pictorialism. For Bach, notes were not
just sounds, but the very stuff of creation. If he could use them to
shape the Cross, or to depict a gesture of Christ's hand, or to suggest the flight of the spirit to heaven, then he was happy. For
example, take this recitative later on in the *Passion:*

Soloist:

And when they had sung a hymn of praise to-ge-ther

Did you hear the slow ascent to the Mount of Olives?

Harpsichord and singer:

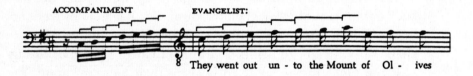

And that is not all. As it continues, listen to the musical commotion that Bach creates to the words "And the sheep of the flock shall be scattered abroad":

Soloist and harpsichord:

And then a lyric image of the Ascension, through another simple scale:

But how different is this scale, with its halo of strings, from the
dry one depicting the ascent to the Mount of Olives!

We begin to see now what the great Albert Schweitzer calls
Bach's "tone-speech," by which he means that mystic fusion of
words and notes that resulted in a whole new Bachian language.
It is in this language that Bach writes his drama, not only in the
recitative sections where the story is being told, but everywhere
in the *Passion*.

For instance, there now comes a chorale which is heard no
fewer than five times throughout the course of the work, a beautiful melody:

Piano:

Each time this chorale appears, it is presented in a new way: with
different words, in different keys, and with different harmoniza-
tions. And through these differences of tone-speech, Bach is able
to communicate a variety of meanings that is phenomenal.

In this first appearance of the chorale, the words are "Acknowl-
edge me, my Keeper, my Shepherd," referring to the sheep in the
preceding recitation. The harmonic setting is, therefore, simple
and pastoral. The inner voices move scalewise, with no ornamen-
tal skips or elaborate counterpoint:

Chorus:

But, at the moment when Jesus dies, the chorale is heard again in a very different arrangement. The words are now: "When I, too, am departing, then part Thou not from me." Accordingly, the harmonies are now brooding, chromatic, mysteriously twisted with suffering, and darkened by the presence of death:

Chorus:

This is one of the most awe-inspiring moments in all music. But then, almost every moment in the *Passion* is awe-inspiring. Over and over again, Bach gives us this magic through his extraordinary unity of words and music.

For example, in the Gethsemane scene, when Jesus finds his disciples sleeping, He says: "What, could ye not watch with Me one hour? Watch ye, and pray ye enter not into temptation." And he continues:

Soloist and strings:

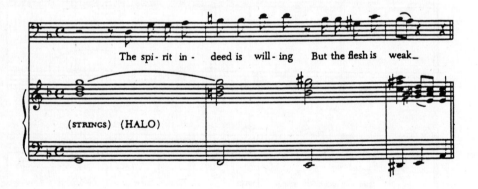

How wonderful is the setting of that word *weak!* You are expecting a normal resolution of the harmony:

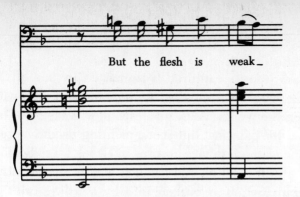

But Bach paints the word for us by an irresolute chord:

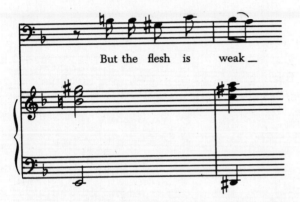

Can you feel the "weakness" of the harmony?

And, as for word-painting, nothing excels the moment of betrayal, when Judas kisses his master. The kiss, with all its fake sweetness, is made almost visual to us, in an overromanticized phrase:

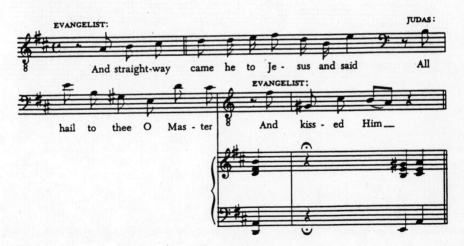

The moment when Jesus is captured is signalized by one of the great pieces of the whole work, a duet for soprano and alto, with choral backing, on the words "Alas, my Jesus now is taken." This is no longer just word-painting, but scene-painting on the largest scale. It is like one of those great choruses in Greek tragedy. The two solo singers are like the chorus leaders; and as their contrapuntal lament spins out, it is broken into by startling cries of "Leave Him, bind Him not!" from the chorus of disciples:

Duet and chorus:

Then as the soloists sing, "He's led away. Ah, they have bound
Him," we hear heavy measured treads in the orchestra, as of
inexorable footsteps:

Duet and orchestra:

And then it all erupts in a tremendous choral outburst, calling on
the lightning and thunder to destroy these murderers. After hearing this fugal chorus, you can never again say that counterpoint is
dull. This is drama at the boiling point:

Double Chorus:

Pure drama, on the highest level— the Bachian level. And on through the work, with unbelievable consistency, this level is maintained, as in the moment when Pontius Pilate offers the mob their choice of Barabbas or Jesus to be released:

Soloists and chorus:

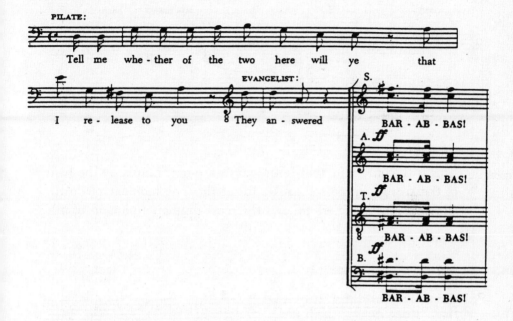

Or the last, heart-breaking moment on the Cross:

Soloists:

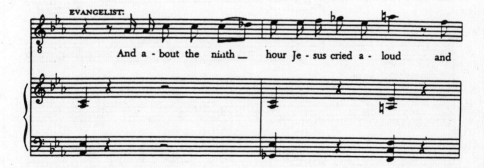

This is the only time that Jesus' words are not framed by the halo of the strings. A master stroke, for at this one moment of death, Christ is mortal. There follows the most dramatic moment of all:

Soloist and orchestra:

And then the final chorus— the farewell to Christ in the tomb, like a great, exalted lullaby:

Chorus:

Oh, if it were only possible to show you all the wonders of this work! But they are infinite. Nobody knows them all, even with a lifetime of study. And think that this is only one work in the vast catalogue of Bach's output, one volume among all these dozens:

(L. B. shows the complete edition of Bach's works, forty-odd huge volumes)

songs, dances, suites, partitas, sonatas, toccatas, preludes, fugues, cantatas, oratorios, masses, passions, fantasias, concertos, chorales, variations, motets, passacaglias— the white-hot creation of fifty ceaseless years.

And what is it that holds all these pages together, that makes it all inevitably the product of one man? The religious spirit. For Bach, all music was religion; writing it was an act of faith; and performing it was an act of worship. Every note was dedicated to

God and to nothing else. And this was true of *all* his music, no matter how secular its purpose. The six *Brandenburg Concertos* for orchestra were technically dedicated to the Margrave of Brandenburg, but the notes praise God, not the Margrave. Every last cello suite or violin sonata, every prelude and fugue from *The Well-Tempered Clavier* praises God.

This is the spine of Bach's work: simple faith. Otherwise, how could he have ever turned out all that glorious stuff to order, meeting deadlines, and carrying on so many simultaneous activities? He played the organ, directed the choir, taught school, instructed his army of children, attended board meetings, kept his eye out for better-paying jobs. Bach was a man, after all, not a god; but he was a man *of* God, and his godliness informs his music from first to last.

WHAT MAKES
OPERA GRAND?

TELECAST: MARCH 23, 1958

(Leonard Bernstein on bare stage)

Here we are in an empty opera house, the great Metropolitan of
New York. It's absolutely bare, stripped of its glamour, its op-
ulence. There are no first-nighters in white ties, no furs, no dia-
monds, no standees screaming, *"Brava, divina!"* There are no
Egyptian temples, no bull rings or Spanish fortresses on this stage.
There are only some Met singers and the Met orchestra.

We're turning this opera house into a laboratory for this one
Sunday afternoon, where we are going to put a microscope on
opera— on *grand* opera— and try to find out what makes it grand.

Grand? What an odd word to use with opera! What does it
mean? Well, to most people it means just that glamour, that op-
ulence, those furs and diamonds. It means a high-toned enterprise,
dedicated to the upper classes, expensive, remote, difficult, silly,
intelligible only to musicians, loved by some lunatic fans— but, in
any case, only for the very few. But oh, how wrong this is!

As a matter of fact, opera is for the *many* and has always been. It is first and foremost a *popular* art. In Italy, cradle of opera, the same people go to hear *Aïda* as to watch a soccer game. All over Europe, going to the opera is simply going to the theater. Opera is theater, even a more popular form of theater because it is so emotionally direct. There is no way in all theater of making the simple statement "I love you" as strongly as having a tenor come right down to the footlights and belt out:

L. B. walks to the footlights and sings:

It is of a monolithic simplicity. The basic human emotions are pinpointed and magnified 'way beyond life size so that you can't miss them. Each emotion comes at you gigantically, in a clear, direct, uncluttered, full-blown way. For example, let's take a basic human emotion: love.

(At this point the second-act love duet from Wagner's Tristan and Isolde *is performed.)*

Now that's as passionate as anyone can get, within the bounds of decency. Where else in all theater can you find love so grandly isolated and amplified? No statement of that white-hot flame has ever equaled Wagner's statement of it in sheer magnitude: a love scene that takes up almost two thirds of the whole act. But the magnitude of this greatest of all love duets does not stem only from its size. It is also enormous in its expressive power, its scope, its variety. The music ranges all the way from the most intimate murmurings:

L.B. plays piano and sings:

through serene lyric passages:

to breathless questioning:

to transported phrases where the lovers overlap each other's phrases in their almost delirious impatience:

Molto vivo

until, finally, it reaches that unbelievable passage of ascending sequences where it seems that there is no limit to how high this passion can soar.

You see what enormous variety there is.

One of the chief reasons for the tremendously direct power of opera is that it is *sung*. Now, that fact may seem childishly obvious, but it acquires great significance when you consider that of all the different instruments in this vast, heterogeneous collection called an orchestra, there is none that can compete in any way with the sublime expressivity of the human voice. It is the greatest instrument there is; and when such a voice, or several, or many together, carry the weight of a drama, of a story line, of an emotional situation, then there is nothing in all theater to compare with it for sheer immediacy of impact.

Think of the emotion of jealousy as it is operaticized in the last act of *Carmen:*

Soprano and tenor at piano:

That's jealousy in spades. Or think of hope, as in the final trio from *Faust:*

Soprano, tenor, basso, piano:

Or take the opposite of hope— despair, as we hear it in Moussorgsky's masterpiece, *Boris Godunov:*

Basso and piano:

God, a - bove Who de - sir - eth not the sin - ner's death

Have mer - cy up - on me, On

me the guil - ty Tsar Bo - ris

Or when Strauss's Salome sings her exaltation of evil after kissing
the decapitated head of John the Baptist, we are left crawling
with the sense of sin:

Soprano and piano:

Now, all these primary emotions are not merely presented to us; they are *hurled* at us. You see, music is something terribly special. It doesn't have to pass through the censor of the brain before it can reach the heart; it goes directly to the heart. You don't have to screen it, as you do words in a play. An F-sharp doesn't have to be considered in the mind; it is a direct hit, and, therefore, all the more powerful. Think of Shakespeare's King Lear in an opera. He'd be raging as no Lear ever could rage in the spoken play: in a great bass voice, with a frantic, high G-flat, with a howling chorus offstage, and ninety players helping him in the pit. Of course, in a play, where there are only words to listen to, there is more chance for subtlety, and maybe profundity of ideas. There is more time to bandy words about, more chance to examine and re-examine, rationalize and justify, as for instance Iago does in *Othello*. As a result, Shakespeare's Iago comes out a subtler and more controversial figure than would an operatic Iago. Shakespeare's character is not exactly a villain, yet he indulges in villainous actions. He is certainly the "heavy" of the play, and yet his motives can be explained in any number of ways, some of which he explains himself in his various soliloquies, as, for example, this one:

Actor recites Iago's Soliloquy:

> "That Cassio loves her, I do well believe it;
> That she loves him, 'tis apt and of great credit;
> The Moor, howbeit that I endure him not,
> Is of a constant, loving, noble nature;
> And I dare think he'll prove to Desdemona
> A most dear husband. Now, I do love her too,
> Not out of absolute lust, though peradventure
> I stand accountant for as great a sin,
> But partly led to diet my revenge,
> For that I do suspect the lusty Moor
> Hath leaped into my seat; the thought whereof
> Doth, like a poisonous mineral, gnaw my inwards;"*

L. B.:

Can you imagine all those words set to music? Never! They are too rational, too self-contradictory, too dependent on the mind for their appeal. In the book of an opera, or the libretto, there is no time for all this rationalization. In opera, the music expands the text to such a degree, emotionally, in time, and in many other ways, that the words must be almost rudimentary in their function. The characters must be boldly carved, uncomplicated, and easy to recognize. The emotional patterns must be equally fundamental. In other words, the operatic Iago has got to be either a good guy or a bad guy, and no shilly-shallying. So that when we go from this fat play *Othello*

(L. B. shows the play)

to this skinny libretto *Otello*

(L. B. shows the libretto)

* The Soliloquy continues for fifteen more lines.

we find a whole other Iago, exactly suited to Verdi's operatic needs. This Iago is a plain, old-fashioned villain. No mystery about him, no complex motivations, no excuses. He is evil, he knows it— and he lets us know it— smack in the face. "*Credo!*" he shouts. "I believe in a cruel God who made me in his image. I believe that man is vile; and I am only a man. I believe that man dies after all his folly, and that after death there is nothing. Heaven is an old-fashioned lie!"

Baritone with orchestra:

So far we have had a glimpse into various bits and kinds of opera, and in every case we have found the same thing to be true: opera is big, bigger than the spoken theater, bigger than life. And what makes it bigger? Music, sung music.

Just how is it that music does this? We're going to find out by taking the entire third act of Puccini's *La Bohème,* a brief but delicious act, and examining it from the viewpoint of what music does to expand mere drama into opera.

The scene is Paris, 1830. We see a tavern, located near one of those toll gates they used to have on the outskirts of the city. It is a gray winter morning, not yet quite dawn. It is snowing; it is very cold. Right away we hear Puccini setting this atmosphere for us in the music: cold, hollow fifths:

L. B. plays opening bars at piano under talk:

Now, there are various ways that cold can be shown on the stage. Snow can fall in the shape of Rinso or Lux, the lighting can be gray and unfriendly, and citizens can go about all muffled to the ears, beating themselves to keep warm. But none of these comes anywhere near the coldness we feel from those cold, empty fifths that Puccini rains like snowflakes over the stage. Against this we hear various frozen-faced workers calling to the custom guards to open the gate and let them into Paris. And, by way of contrast, we will hear singing coming from the tavern— night owls who are still at it, clinking their glasses and whooping it up.

Piano:

Among them is Musetta, singing a fragment of her famous waltz that we heard in Act II:

All this establishes the atmosphere of the act. And how brilliantly
Puccini does it!

*(At this point, the opening of the third act is presented with chorus
and orchestra.)*

Now we've seen the first way music can expand drama into
opera: by expanding the very scenery itself. But now the story
begins. And because we're in a laboratory, we're free to make
experiments; and so we're going to break this story into two versions— a spoken version and the sung version. First you will see
each section acted out in English, by "normal" actors, but in exact
accordance with the libretto; and only then you will hear it sung,
so that you really know what is going on. (But a word of caution:
remember what we said about librettos. They are not plays; they
are poetic skeletons.)

Our story involves four main characters, all Latin Quarter
bohemians: Mimi, the delicate little seamstress, and Rodolfo, the
starving poet, who has recently become her lover. The other loving couple consists of Rodolfo's best pal, Marcello, who is a
painter, and Musetta, a spicy dish who has been living with him.
When we last saw these Greenwich Village types, in Act II, all
was well. They were bathed in love and laughter on Christmas
Eve. But now, apparently, something has gone wrong, as Mimi is
about to tell us.

Actors (speaking):

MIMI:
Excuse me, sir. Can you tell me which is the tavern where a
painter is working?
POLICEMAN *(Points):*
There it is.
MIMI:
Thank you. *(To milkmaid)* Oh, my good woman, would you be so
kind as to call Marcello, the painter? I have to speak with him,
and I have so little time. Tell him— softly— that Mimi is waiting.
(Milkmaid goes inside)

POLICEMAN *(To market woman):*
Hey, what's in that basket? *(Looks)* Empty. Pass.
MARCELLO *(Entering):*
Mimi!
MIMI:
I hoped that I would find you here.
MARCELLO:
Yes, we've been living here rentfree for more than a month.
Musetta sings for the customers, and I paint warriors all over the
façade. It's cold out here. Come in.
MIMI:
Is Rodolfo inside?
MARCELLO:
Yes.
MIMI:
Then I can't go in— no, no!
MARCELLO:
Why not?
MIMI *(Breaking down):*
Oh, good Marcello, help me! Please!
MARCELLO:
What's gone wrong?
MIMI:
Rodolfo has left me out of jealousy. He loves me, but he doesn't
trust me. Any little look or word or gesture I make throws him
into a fit of suspicion and anger. I can even feel him spying on my
dreams at night. Every minute he's shouting, "It's over! You're not
for me! Go take another lover!" Ah, it breaks my heart. Of course
he doesn't mean it, but what is there to answer, Marcello?
MARCELLO:
If you're both so unhappy, you shouldn't live together.
MIMI:
You're right. We should part. But we've tried to so often, and we
can't. Help us, do help us! Would you talk to him?
MARCELLO:
Now take Musetta and me. We're happy because we don't take
our love so seriously. We sing, we laugh— that's the only way.

MIMI:
Marcello, please do your best to help us.
MARCELLO:
All right, all right. I'll talk to him.

L. B.:

Well, now, that's not exactly a plot to set the world on fire. A little lovers' spat, that's all. He's left her; he's jealous; she doesn't know what to do. I imagine you couldn't care less. But now let's have the same scene with Puccini's music, and you will find yourself caring a great deal.

(The same scene is now performed by singers and orchestra.)[*]

L. B.:

Do you find yourself caring about the story? Of course you do. Why? The addition of perfectly glorious music. But it's not just *any* old glorious music. It is carefully planned by a theatrical wizard to take the characters and magnify them for us. For instance, Mimi. From the first note she sings, to the guard at the city gates, the music is telling us how sick she is. Now notice I didn't say the *words* are telling this. All they're saying is "Excuse me, can you tell me," and so forth. Nothing but a plot line. But the music tells us much more:

L. B. sings:

---

[*] The following lines in Italian start the scene.
MIMI:
Sa dirmi, scusi,
Qual' è l'osteria
Dove un pittor lavora?
SERGEANT:
Eccola.
Etc.

You hear all those rests between the phrases? That panting struggle for breath? And, of course, you must have noticed that the whole musical line is constantly falling, giving us an exact sense of her failing strength.

Then, in addressing the milkmaid, she makes a new effort, and the music strains upward:

L. B. sings:

But here, too, the line drops, as her strength wanes. Such perfect sick music! And what makes it even sicker is that the line drops by half tones, by the smallest possible intervals, so that it's almost like one long sigh.

And on top of that, the harmony in the orchestra is a series of descending ninth chords, very sick-sounding indeed.

L. B. plays:

Do you see how all these little elements together conspire to paint Mimi for us in unmistakable musical colors? And all that was not even a melody. It was only recitative, that unfortunate word that usually means nothing of much melodic interest is going on. But since, in grand opera, we are committed to *singing* the whole story from start to finish, there has to be some kind of recitative. An opera can't all be arias and tunes, expressing feelings. That would be completely static. The story has to move. So, in order to tell the story, we're stuck with that bugaboo recitative.* That's the element in opera you're always bored by, or infuriated by, or embarrassed by, because you think everyone but you knows what's being said, and you feel inferior. So much flotsam and jetsam. But when recitative is handled as Puccini does it, making it work for the character, and giving it such musico-dramatic meaning, then it's never boring. It has its own special kind of beauty.

Now on with the play. Marcello has promised to speak to Rodolfo. He sends Mimi away, so as not to cause a scene. But she hides behind a tree and eavesdrops on the conversation of the two friends.

Actors (speaking):

RODOLFO:
Marcello, at last, I can talk to you alone. Marcello, I want to leave Mimi.
MARCELLO:
You certainly change your mind easily.
RODOLFO:
Well, you know how it is. I think it's all over. Then I look into those blue eyes, and I'm all on fire again. I don't know.
MARCELLO:
So you want to start the whole funeral over again?
RODOLFO:
Forever.
MARCELLO:
Why don't you change? What good is love if it's dreary? If love isn't fun, it's hopeless. You're a jealous man.

* *cf.* examples of recitative, pages 154, 155, 156, 157.

RODOLFO:
A little.
MARCELLO:
Jealous, cantankerous, crazy, bigoted, boring and stubborn.
MIMI *(Aside):*
Now Rodolfo will get mad. Ah, what is one to do!
RODOLFO:
That Mimi is a flirt; she plays with men. Some fly-by-night noble-man gives her the eye, and there she is, showing her ankles, en-couraging him.
MARCELLO:
May I say you're not being sincere?
RODOLFO:
All right, then, I'm not. I've been lying, trying to hide my real agony. I love Mimi, more than anything in the world. But I'm so afraid. Mimi is ill and gets worse every day. The poor little thing is finished.
MARCELLO:
Mimi!
MIMI *(Aside):*
What does he mean?
RODOLFO:
She has a terrible, racking cough; she's lost all color in her cheeks.
MARCELLO:
Poor Mimi.
MIMI *(Aside):*
Am I going to die?
RODOLFO:
And my room is a squalid hole— no heat, ice-cold, drafty. She never complains; but I feel so guilty. It's my fault that she's dying.
MARCELLO:
What can we do?
MIMI *(Aside):*
I am going to die!

Now we know the truth: Mimi is fatally ill, and Rodolfo has left her for her own sake. But touching as this situation is, it is nothing compared to the same situation after our wizard has got his hands on it. Listen to how he has taken it and, through music, expanded it in emotional grandeur into a genuinely tragic statement.

*(The same scene is now performed by singers and orchestra.)**

L. B.:

As you see, Puccini's music has actually expanded the size of the emotions. But the secret of this scene's emotional grandeur lies in a typical Puccini master stroke. The whole first part of the conversation is set to music that is superficial and noncommittal. Rodolfo sings with boyish vigor, as though he were not particularly concerned.

L. B. sings:

* The following lines in Italian start the scene.
RODOLFO:
Marcello, finalmente!
Qui niun ci sente.
Io voglio separarmi da Mimi.
MARCELLO:
Sei volubil cosi?
Etc.

It's more like a march, or even a dance— young, energetic, even sarcastic. The friends sound like two college roommates. But this is just what generates the power, because Rodolfo is hiding his true feelings. So that once he breaks down, everything that follows is twice as emotional by contrast. For instance, take the moment when he is lying about why he has left Mimi. "She's a flirt," he says, "and plays with men." He says it to this tune:

But a moment later Marcello challenges his sincerity, and Rodolfo
breaks down and tells the truth, to the exact same tune, but only
with the second note changed, raised to high A:

And what emotion is carried by that one different note! In it is all
the release of truth, the heat of truth bursting from him. Or take
Rodolfo's lines, "She has a terrible cough. Her cheeks are pale," and
so on. A rather clinical statement, however poetic it sounds in
Italian. Puccini might have set it just as clinically, to sort of
neutral music.

L. B. improvises:

But, of course, he doesn't. Instead, he makes Rodolfo sing a marvelous, passionate melody to those words, so that he is not only saying Mimi is sick, but also that he is in torture and despair because of it.

L. B. plays and sings:

di -   san -   gue ha ros -   se   *etc.*

That's what makes opera.

Now we come to a new function of music in opera, another expansion of reality, and that is simultaneous singing. This is one of the great delights of opera: just think of ensemble numbers like the Quartet from *Rigoletto*, the Sextet from *Lucia*, the Trio from *Der Rosenkavalier*. And why are these always the high points of opera? Because they provide a thrill that no other art form can provide: the thrill of being able to hear several emotional statements at once. You could never do it in a play. People just can't speak simultaneously— that is, if they want to be heard. It would only be a jumble, like this next moment in *La Bohème*.

Actors speak simultaneously:

MIMI:	MARCELLO:	RODOLFO:
Oh God, oh God.	What a tragedy!	Mimi is a delicate
It's all over.	The poor thing.	flower, and she needs
My life is finished.	Poor little Mimi.	attention. And I
Oh God, must I die?	What a pity, *etc.*	have nothing but love
Oh God, *etc.*		to give her, *etc.*

L. B.:

A mess. But music accomplishes the miracle, because notes are born to sound together, as words are not. And so this little trio becomes a moment of striking beauty, instead of a jumble. Reality has been expanded by music into a richness of lyricism whereby we can actually perceive three emotions at the same time.

Rodolfo's despair:

Marcello's mumbling helplessness:

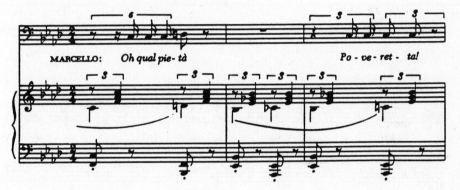

And over it all, Mimi's little gasps of anguish:

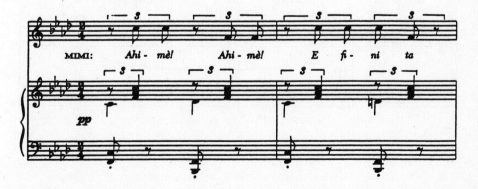

Together, they make a network of emotions that is in itself a new kind of emotional experience:

Trio sings:

Do you see what I mean by "network of emotions"? That's something only opera can give you.

Now let's see what happens next in our story.

Actors (speaking):

(Mimi's coughing betrays her presence.)

RODOLFO:

Mimi . . . what's this? You're here? You heard me?

MARCELLO:

She's heard everything.

RODOLFO:

Darling, don't worry. You know me. I get upset over nothing. Come in where it's warm.

MIMI:

No, the smell in there would stifle me.

RODOLFO:

Ah, Mimi.

(Musetta laughs offstage)
MARCELLO:
That's Musetta laughing. Who's she laughing with? That little flirt; I'll show you.
(Marcello exits into tavern)

L. B.:

A bit of action, no more. Watch and see how here, in still another way, music makes it big. Each of those little actions is spotlighted and strengthened by the way the music refers to familiar themes from the preceding acts. For instance, when Rodolfo comforts Mimi, trying to make light of what he said, he does it to the melody of Mimi's first aria in Act I:

L. B. plays piano:

When she says, "No, I can't bear the stench in there," it is to the theme of her illness:

When Musetta is heard laughing, the orchestra gives us the Musetta theme:

This technique of so-called *leitmotiv* composing, or tagging every character with a musical label, reached its height with Wagner and its bottom in Hollywood movie scores. But when it is used well, it can do wonders, as in this very scene.

*(The foregoing section is sung.)**

---

*The following lines in Italian start the section.

RODOLFO:
Chè?! Mimì! Tu qui?
MARCELLO:
Ella dunque ascoltava?!
Etc.

L. B.:

Now we come to one of the chief ways in which music expands drama, in sheer physical time. And this is what I meant by opera creating its own time, its own fourth dimension. Let's compare the timing of this next scene, spoken and sung, on our watches. Here it is spoken.

Actors (speaking):

MIMI:

Goodbye.

RODOLFO:

What? You're going?

MIMI:

Once I flew happily from my nest at the sound of your love call. Now I'm going back again. Goodbye, with no bitterness. Listen. Put together whatever few things I've left around the room— my little gold locket, my prayerbook— just wrap them all in an apron, and I'll send for them tomorrow. And, listen, under the pillow you'll find the little bonnet you bought me last Christmas. If you like, you can keep it as a souvenir of our love. Goodbye, and no bitterness.

L. B.:

Now that took exactly 36 seconds. But emotionally it should take much longer, because the moment is so terribly important to them both. It doesn't seem so important in the spoken version: "Goodbye— no hard feelings— " finished. But underneath those apparently light words flows a deep current of feeling. And so Puccini stops time and gives Mimi an aria to sing. The words are no different, or more numerous. But they are said in a new dimension, so that what was said about a locket and a pink bonnet suddenly acquires a big, new meaning. It is Mimi's renunciation of a great love, of her entire life.

*(Mimi sings the "Addio")**

L. B.:

Now that took 210 seconds. And what golden seconds they were, because in them time stopped. There were *no* minutes, *no* seconds. We have been suspended in a moment of great emotion, and the fact that that moment lasted 210 seconds is of no importance. For us it has been both a moment and an eternity.

Finally we have the remainder of the act: the wonderful duet between the lovers, followed by the wonderful quartet of the two couples, one couple fighting like cats, the other mooning over their reconciliation.

Actors (speaking):

RODOLFO:
Then it's really over. You're going, my little one. Goodbye to all my dreams of love.
MIMI:
Goodbye to the sweet waking in the mornings.

---

* The following lines in Italian start the section.
MIMI:
Addio.
RODOLFO:
Che! Vai?
MIMI:
Donde lieta usci al tuo grido d'amore.
Etc.

RODOLFO:
Goodbye to the smile I had dreamed of all my life.
MIMI:
Goodbye to jealousy.
RODOLFO:
Kisses . . .
MIMI:
Bitterness . . .
RODOLFO:
Poetry . . .
MIMI:
To be alone in winter! It's like dying.
RODOLFO:
Alone in winter— it is like dying.
BOTH:
But in spring, there's always the sun to keep us company.
MARCELLO *(Offstage)*:
What were you doing? What were you saying?
MUSETTA *(Offstage)*:
How dare you!
MARCELLO *(Offstage)*:
I saw you with that man . . .
MUSETTA *(Offstage)*:
That's enough.
MIMI:
In spring no one's alone.
MARCELLO *(Entering)*:
You changed color when I came in.
MUSETTA *(Entering)*:
That man was only asking me to dance.
Simultaneously:

RODOLFO:	MARCELLO:
You can talk with	You little flirt.
lilies and roses.	MUSETTA:
MIMI:	And I said: "There's nothing
There is a sweet	I like better than dancing."

chirping coming
from the nests.
RODOLFO:
When spring comes,
there is the sun to
keep you company.
MIMI:
Fountains are chattering.
RODOLFO:
The evening breezes
comfort your pain.
MIMI:
Let's wait until it's
spring again. I'm yours
for always.
(*They start to go*)
RODOLFO:
Let's not part from each
other until the spring.
MIMI:
Until the spring.
Somehow I wish winter
would last forever.
(*They exit*)

MARCELLO:
There was more to it than that.
MUSETTA:
I must have my freedom.
MARCELLO:
I'll kill you if I catch you.
MUSETTA:
Listen to him. We're not married.
I hate a lover who acts like a husband.
MARCELLO:
I'm no toy you can play with.
MUSETTA:
I'll act the way I please. If you
don't like it, goodbye.
MARCELLO:
You're going? I'm delighted.
What luck!
BOTH:
Goodbye. The pleasure's all mine.
MUSETTA (*Exiting*):
You house painter!
MARCELLO:
Snake!
MUSETTA:
Toad! (*Exits*)
MARCELLO:
Witch! (*Follows her out*)

L. B.:

Well, that's not much of a story. The lovers have decided not to separate after all, at least until spring. So what? But this story with Puccini's music becomes one of the most touching episodes in the history of theater. In it you will hear used all the devices we have spoken of: music expanding words, situations, atmosphere, character, emotion. Time is also expanded; leitmotivs are used, and, of course, simultaneous singing. And, in addition to all these, you will hear the most dramatic device of simultaneous

contrast, with the two duets pitted against each other, one broadly
lyrical and the other agitated and fussy. This is really the crowning delight of opera: that in the very same moment we can experience conflicting passions, contrasting moods and separate events.
And because only the gods have ever been able to perceive more
than one thing at a time, we are, for this short period, raised to the
level of the gods.

(Quartet with orchestra performs the foregoing section)[*]

L. B. returns to stage:

What we have been seeing today is the innocence of opera, the—
well— almost *naïveté* of the way in which emotions are magnified
and crystallized. We have seen how music takes the mere words
of drama and gives them new heights and new depths. That is the
real meaning of the "grand" in grand opera.

But music can go even a step further: it can render words almost unimportant. This is the highest estate opera can reach,
where the music is so communicative that the merest general
knowledge of the dramatic action is enough to give you the key to
a rich enjoyment of the work. When operatic music is great, it
creates its own special world, within which time and space are
revised, and even meaning is metamorphosed, and presented on a
different level. Therefore the measure of its greatness is the extent
to which it makes you an inhabitant of its own special world— the
extent to which it invites you in and lets you breathe its strange,
other-planet air. With the greatest operas— the *Don Giovannis* and
Tristans and *Otellos* and *Rosenkavaliers* and *Wozzecks*— we enter

---

[*] The following lines in Italian start the section.
RODOLFO:
Dunque è proprio finita? Te ne vai, te ne vai; la mia piccina?
Etc.

fully into such a world; and when we come out we are enriched
and ennobled.

(Here followed a performance of the final scene of Tristan and
Isolde, *with which the telecast concluded.)*

MUSIC CREDITS

Leonard Bernstein, composer, conductor, pianist, teacher, and writer, was born August 25, 1918. Among his accomplishments, he served from 1957 to 1969 as conductor and music director of the New York Philharmonic, inaugurated two seminal television series on the performing arts, "Young People's Concerts" and "Omnibus," and lectured and mentored extensively on musical subjects. Books by Mr. Bernstein include *Leonard Bernstein's Young People's Concerts, Findings, The Joy of Music,* and *The Unanswered Question*. Leonard Bernstein died on October 14, 1990.

"Life without music is unthinkable,
Music without life is academic.
That is why my contact with music is a total embrace."
—LEONARD BERNSTEIN, *Findings*

Award winners . . . bestsellers . . . familiar favorites . . . twentieth-century classics. Leonard Bernstein's unforgettable music-making can be heard on over 100 audio and video recordings in Deutsche Grammophon's renowned catalogue.

Among Our Highlights:

Bernstein: *West Side Story*—Te Kanawa/Carreras/Troyanos/Bernstein
Bernstein: *Candide*—Anderson/Hadley/Ludwig/Bernstein
    Grammy winner!
Bernstein in Berlin—Bernstein's historic performance of Beethoven's Ninth Symphony in East Berlin on Christmas Day 1989, celebrating the fall of the Wall.
Bernstein: Final Concert—Beethoven's Seventh Symphony and Britten's "4 Sea Interludes" from *Peter Grimes;* Bernstein/Boston Symphony at Tanglewood on August 19, 1990.
Mahler: Symphonies—Bernstein/New York Philharmonic/Concertgebouw Orchestra/London Symphony/Vienna Philharmonic

For a **free discography** of Leonard Bernstein's Deutsche Grammophon recordings, write to: Bernstein Recordings, Deutsche Grammophon, PolyGram Classics and Jazz, 825 Eighth Avenue, New York, NY 10019, or fax your request to: 212-333-8402.

For other inquiries please write to: The Leonard Bernstein Society, Department G, 25 Central Park West, Suite 1-Y, New York, NY 10023.